Contents

Discipline in schools

Editor Barry Turner

7 1973

9

6

Ward Lock|Educational

ISBN 0 7062 3149 x casebound
ISBN 0 7062 3150 3 paperback (pbk)

Set in 11 on 12 point Georgian Linotype
by Willmer Brothers Limited, Birkenhead
for Ward Lock Educational
116 Baker Street, London WIM 2BB
Made in England

Introduction

The idea behind *Discipline in Schools* is not to put across a single point of view about the proper definition of school discipline but to bring together contrasting opinions and attitudes so that the reader can be given the groundwork on which to base his own conclusions.

Discipline is one of the most controversial topics in education. It is an area of interest that closely involves many parents and teachers who feel the need to redefine school values to take account of changes in the social environment but are not always sure of the best way to go about the job. Should we move further in the direction of Neill's Summerhill, allowing near total freedom to youngsters to find their own philosophy of behaviour and belief, or would it be wiser to seek to preserve some or all of the traditional standards as an essential bulwark against the risks of social disruption?

The contributors to this book are teachers, academics or parents and some of them combine two or all three of these functions. Their individual approach to the question is linked to the need to give practical advice to those who are just beginning a teaching career or to parents who are wondering how to establish a relationship with their children that is satisfying to both sides. The book does not attempt to solve all the problems of the generation gap but it does point the way to some possible solutions.

Barry Turner 1973

Catherine Storr

Family view

Since I was a child several words which were formerly never used in polite society have become acceptable, and are spoken and printed without raising more than the occasional eyebrow; no need for me to reproduce them here, any reader can supply them for himself. But at the same time, through what I suspect is a sort of law of natural selection, which keeps our vocabulary perpetually on the move, but at the same time fairly constant in size, while we gain new words we also lose old ones. Several which used to be perfectly admissible have been outlawed, and this change, like the other, represents a change in our attitudes. We have become more permissive about sex and more democratic, in theory if not in practice. The lip service we pay to concepts of antiracialism and equal opportunities for all has made words like 'wog' and 'nigger' obscene, and in our anxiety to dissociate ourselves from the reactionary, backward-looking brigade, we are unwilling to use dirty words like 'social class', 'punishment' and 'discipline'.

Just as our grandparents seem to have assumed that if you do not name the sexual organs or sexual practice they will cease to exist – at any rate in the very young, and in the case of girls until they emerge, like Pallas Athene, fully armed on the wedding night – so by refusing to employ these previously harmless conjunctions of letters we are pretending to an ideal but unrealistic state of affairs. Although I believe that to call the insane 'mentally ill' rather than 'lunatic' does represent a more sympathetic attitude, and that to say 'coloured' is less denigrating than the old contemptuous 'nigger', these verbal shifts towards a more compassionate and fraternal state of mind do not prevent many people from taking violently prejudiced stands against others who are 'different' in some way from the norm, whether it is in their emotional responses or in the colour of their skin. In the same way, although we have progressed a little way towards a better understanding of the working of the child's mind, it would be too optimistic to suppose that by refusing to speak of the necessity for discipline, or even for punishment, we are going to rear a generation of painlessly socialized, sensible, liberal-minded children.

Why do we not want to believe that discipline is any longer necessary to achieve this much desired end? One of the answers lies in our exaggerated respect for science and in what it can accomplish. We are so used to the idea that with the help of the advances of modern medicine we can avoid the ills that plagued our ancestors – no need now to fear smallpox, bubonic plague, typhoid, tuberculosis, whooping cough, polio – that we begin to believe that if only we attend to the precepts of the specialists on child psychology, we ought to be able to raise, without the necessity for corrective measures, a race of super children. But in thinking this, we forget several vital issues. To begin with, psychology is not a science in the sense that mathematics, physics, chemistry are sciences. It is, perhaps, the misfortune of psychology that its first great exponent, Freud, was trained in the strict school of neurology, and desired above everything to put his important and extraordinary observations on the same respectable level. But, in spite of sometimes being called 'The Science of Behaviour', psychology is not in the same class as the exact sciences; the human mind is still a largely uncharted sea, and although certain precepts have been laid down – and accepted as dogma by enthusiastic disciples – they are really no more than hypotheses. They need still to be tested and tried out, and we should regard them with caution rather than with absolute faith, ready to discard them when they prove inadequate or absolutely wrong. An amusing example of how often the theories of child psychologists have been taken as law by one generation of parents, only to be refuted or ignored by the next, is given by Anna Freud (1966):

> ... it did not take more than one or two decades of such (psycho-analytic) work before a number of analytic authors ventured beyond the boundaries of fact finding and began to apply the new

knowledge to the upbringing of children. The therapeutic analyses of adult neurotics left no doubt about the detrimental influence of many parental and environmental attitudes and actions such as dishonesty in sexual matters, unrealistically high moral standards, overstrictness or overindulgence, frustrations, punishments, or seductive behaviour.

The sequence of these extrapolations is well known by now. Thus, at a time when psychoanalysts laid great emphasis on the seductive influence of sharing the parents' bed and the traumatic consequences of witnessing parental intercourse, parents were warned against bodily intimacy with their children and against performing the sexual act in the presence of even their youngest infants. When it was proved in the analyses of adults that the witholding of sexual knowledge was responsible for many intellectual inhibitions, full sexual enlightenment at an early age was advocated. When hysterical symptoms, frigidity, impotence etc were traced back to prohibitions and the subsequent repressions of sex in childhood, psychoanalytic upbringing put on its programme a lenient and permissive attitude towards the manifestations of infantile, pregenital sexuality. When the new instinct theory gave aggression the status of a basic drive, tolerance was extended also to the child's early and violent hostilities, his death wishes against parents and siblings etc. When anxiety was recognized as playing a central part in symptom formation, every effort was made to lessen the children's fear of parental authority. When guilt was shown to correspond to the tension between the inner agencies, this was followed by the ban on all educational measures likely to produce a severe super-ego. . . . Finally in our own time, when analytic investigations have turned to earliest events in the first year of life and highlighted their importance, these specific insights are being translated into new and in some respects revolutionary techniques of infant care.

Some of the pieces of advice given to parents over the years were consistent with each other; others were contradictory and mutually exclusive. . . . Above all to rid the child of anxiety proved an impossible task. Parents did their best to reduce the children's fear of them, merely to find that they were increasing guilt feelings, i.e. fears of the child's own conscience. Where, in its turn, the severity of the super-ego was reduced, children produced the deepest of all anxieties, i.e. the fear of human beings who feel unprotected against the pressure of their drives.

In short, in spite of many partial advances, psychoanalytic education did not succeed in becoming the preventive measure that it had set out to be. It is true that the children who grew up under its influence were in some respects different from earlier generations, but they were not freer from anxiety or from conflicts, and therefore not less exposed to neurotic or other mental illnesses.

Coupled with the hope that by attending to the specialists we should be able to dispense with any corrective measures, has been our growing dislike for those measures in themselves. This, I think, is due largely to our need to prove ourselves truly democratic, not only in respect of social levels, but also in respect of age. Our confidence that age and experience bring wisdom has been badly shaken. The days of 'Father knows best' are over; father will only know best if he has read the appropriate books on child development, and these will, nowadays, tell him more of the terrible results of his slightest mistake than give him actual down to earth rulings. He will also learn that since any failings on the child's part are likely to be the direct consequence of the parents' misdoings, punishment is inappropriate and will probably lead only to further traumata. So, without the backing of authority, actuated in the main by the desire to do the best we can by our children, we try to side with them, to understand instead of condemning, to explain instead of scolding, in fact to eliminate the gap made between us by the years. I am convinced that one of the main reasons for our dislike of assuming authority and all that it entails is the current fashion for youth. Quite simply, we are afraid of being ranged on the side of the last generation. We do not want to admit the possibility that we are OLD.

I would like to add here, in a sort of parenthesis, that there is another confusing element in the picture, which is connected with the fallacy of supposing that child education is a science when in fact it is more like an art. We seem to hope that, like painting by numbers, if we only follow the instructions closely enough we shall be able to produce a masterpiece. But whereas when you set yourself to practise

4

a technique with inanimate objects, guided by a do-it-yourself hand-book, you probably start and continue in a fairly rational frame of mind, able to take advantage of the advice given, the same is not true of child care. The practice advocated here is concerned with dynamic rather than static situations. I am always astonished at the assumption people appear to make, about other human relationships as well as those between parents and children, that if we *know* what we should do, that is all that is necessary, as if we were computers which, if the information is correctly fed in, must come up with the right responses. Not at all. Every parent and teacher will recognize the feeling of *knowing*, or having at least a shrewd idea of what he or she ought to do in a given situation, and of *not doing it*. A mother may know very well that when Peter hits his baby sister over the head for the eighteenth time, it is not that he is nothing but a murderous little bully, but that he wants more love from his mother; but it is hardly the moment when his mother feels an overflowing love for her jealous little boy, and though she may have been able for the first ten or twelve times to control her irritation – and her despair at her own inadequacy as a parent – the moment will probably come when she will allow herself to forget the textbooks and the warnings, and she will shout. If she is sufficiently hard pressed she may scream or even hit him. Children are not the only creatures who are not always amenable to reason; the adults who are responsible for their upbring-ing also get tired and cross, have their weaknesses and their prejudices and are sometimes simply unable to put into practice the theories they have learned.

Considering all these factors which have brought the idea of dis-cipline into its present state of disrepute, each of us who finds himself even temporarily in authority over another person or persons, has to try to decide what his own attitude is towards it; what he thinks it means, whether or not he is going to employ it, if so how, and finally how it is to be implemented. And it is often this last question which springs first to people's minds. When they hear the word 'discipline' what occurs to them is the enforcement of discipline, in fact punish-ment, which has also contributed to make the former an unneces-sarily dirty word. But this is not what discipline, in the first instance, means. Discipline is, as I see it, the structure, the scheme which is designed to facilitate the smooth working of some activity, whether this is the acquisition of knowledge by the student, the skill of the craftsman, the training of the professional soldier or the rearing and education of children. In order to reach the best possible end in each of these, energy has to be harboured and canalized, time must be measured and allocated and many of man's normal impulses temporarily curbed. The student will have to spend more time with books and less with girls or games than he would probably choose if he followed nothing but his fancy. The craftsman has to learn to overcome man's natural inertia, to ignore distractions and to practise, often with little encouragement, the technique which is a necessary part of his art. The soldier has to be taught to ignore his inborn instinct for self-preservation at all costs, as well as his disinclination to murder. In the same way, since babies are without exception asocial, demanding, selfish little egoists, discipline is needed to subdue their natural egocentrism so that they can live in and with society.

Probably no one would quarrel with this aspect of discipline. It is not fashionable; at present the emphasis is more on the unformulated, the unexpected – in fact the 'happening' – than on the old strict formulae. But discipline is tolerated where it is self-imposed. The trouble begins when the pressure is all from without. It is the idea of one person disciplining another that is so obnoxious to this egalitarian age, even when the person on whom discipline is imposed is too young or, for whatever reason, unable to administer it himself. Because most of us want to retain society more or less in its present form, we reluctantly agree to the enforcement of laws which protect it and us, and it is the easier to do this because in most cases we do not have to take a personal part in the business. Where we cannot but be involved, though, is in the smaller society of the family or the school, and here, whatever the psychoanalytically conscious, intellectual, middle class, anxious parent believes in theory, I am glad to think than in practice, exhaustion and self-defence eventually drive him to formulate some sort of structure of discipline on which family life is run.

It must be clear by now that I am on the side of the disciplinarians. I am for rules. Rules save time; to know what you may or may not do in given circumstances allows great economy of energy and removes a lot of destructive indecision and muddle. Rules represent order; and however anarchic we may feel, we need order, if only that we can rebel against it. One reason, I am convinced, for the dissatisfaction of the young today with the society and family pattern in which they have grown up is that there have not been enough hard and fast lines to give them security. They have found themselves growing up in an atmosphere of adult uncertainty which leaves them bewildered; growing up is never an easy business, and one essential factor in it is a reassessment of the standards of one's elders. If these standards are woolly and indefinite, the adolescent feels cheated. How can he define his own position in relation to something which has so little form and which shifts from moment to moment? Perhaps we all, at any age, retain something of what all small children feel – that an absence of rules implies an absence of care, even of love. A friend of mine once told me that she had tried – too hard – to be the perfect mother to her only, much wanted daughter, born to her late in life, and had made do with the absolute minimum of rules, had supervised her goings and comings as little as possible, never insisting that she come home from evenings out at any fixed hour. Her reward, she told me sadly, was that when she expressed sympathy on behalf of her daughter's girl friend who always had to be in the house by ten o'clock, her daughter remarked, 'Oh I don't know. At least she feels that her mother cares.'

The mistake this woman made, and which so many of us make as parents is, I think, that whereas we recognize the need for some sort of frame of discipline where numbers of people are concerned, it does not seem so necessary in the context of the family. Indeed here our discipline is apt to be mostly empirical; we make up the rules as we go along. Yet even here the pressures of society and the number of external influences which threaten the long infancy of the human child force us to impose certain basic commands. Even those of us who do not insist on such things as 'Say pardon', 'Wipe your mouth', 'Don't touch yourself there', will still be strict about 'Look right, look left, look right again', 'Don't accept lifts from a stranger', 'Keep away from the fire'. If the child can accept these rules before he is old enough to understand why we have made them, I do not see that he cannot also accept others which may not be made to preserve life, but which do oil the sometimes groaning machinery of family life. The trouble, of course, is that the parents, when they make arbitrary rules for their own convenience, rather than to promote the child's health or well-being, are apt to feel guilty. They can accept that external situations over which they have no control, like illness or lack of funds, may render impossible the ideal conditions which Jane Austen's Isabella Knightley – sister to Emma – desired for her children – 'the immediate enjoyment of her little ones ... their having instantly all the liberty and attendance, all the eating and drinking, and sleeping and playing, which they could possibly wish for, without the smallest delay.' What the modern parent cannot accept is the longer view which might show them that immediate gratification can be less important than an equilibrium in which not only the children but also the adults have rights.

One of the difficulties here is that we do not start as we shall have to go on. The tiny baby must be allowed to make demands which disrupt the parents' life, disturbing their work, their occupations and their sleep. At what point, then, should they begin to teach him to contain his hunger or his fright or his desire, at five o'clock in the morning, for a friendly conversation? The answer must vary from child to child and from family to family. Some children suffer more than others from night terrors, some are sound sleepers, others are not; there are no fixed rules. Parents have to try to be flexible, and to match the régime to the individuals contained within it; but remembering that their convenience is also worth consideration. They will be foredoomed to failure also, I think, if they make their rules *in spite of* instead of *on account of* their convictions. If, while believing that the child is owed total liberty, they protect themselves from time to time with instant, occasional rules, these will tend to be too arbitrary, too much the result of an immediate, intolerable situation, and will lapse once the crisis is over. This means that the child becomes confused by laws which appear out of nowhere and sink again without trace; behaviour which aroused no comment before has suddenly been outlawed. What could happen next time? The parents, having acted against their own code, are apologetic, and this makes their behaviour inconsistent. I think this is absolutely wrong.

What I see as one of the main duties of any parent is to try to equip the child for living and for getting as much as possible out of life. For most of us, this means life in some sort of society. We have got to teach the child how to benefit from the advantages of being a social animal, and one of these lessons will be that in order to get the advantages, certain sacrifices have to be made. We shall probably hope to teach him not to accept all the values of any current society without question, but at the same time to forego rebellion simply for rebellion's sake. His first taste of society will be the experience of being a member of the family, and it is here that he will imbibe the first and most impressive lessons. If he is taught that his wants are paramount, that his parents' duty is only to provide him with what he wants at the expense of their own personal lives – and this applies just as much to a family with two or three other children as to an only child – how is he to learn that people other than himself have the right to be considered? The child brought up by parents who are totally permissive has just as much difficulty in adjusting to society outside his home as the child who is brought up at the other extreme, by parents who totally disregard his rights as a person and who think only of themselves. In neither case has the child been shown how to cope, except by extreme measures, with what the rules of society are all about – the conflict between the rights of one individual and those of another. It is only by seeing that his parents consider others and are prepared to consider themselves too, that he can learn how to make this adjustment himself. There will be other fringe benefits. I believe it was sensible Dr Spock who was the first of writers on child care to point out the advantages to both mother and baby if their relationship could be enjoyed – not just tolerated or made the subject of hard work and sacrifice – by both. Different people enjoy different things. Here too we should not take for granted that what suits the friends we admire for their successful families will necessarily suit us. Some parents can enjoy their children only if they are beautifully dressed, beautifully mannered; others prefer them to be unrestrained in voice and mess and self-expression, and I have known families of both kinds which have produced nice, considerate, intelligent, interesting children. The most important thing is that the parents should be confident about the set-up, confident that, in spite of the friction, the occasional blazing row, the normal problems of communal living, they have found – or are finding, since it has to be an infinitely flexible process – a compromise solution which is tolerable if not ideal. Where the parents feel this sort of security, the children are likely to follow suit. They may kick against the rules, may, in later life, discover that they were trivial, expressions of the parents' weaknesses rather than founded on logic or necessity; but I believe that this is less damaging to the child's adult personality and powers of development than where there has been great licence and great material prodigality without the vital factor of respect. Parents who respect the child, from a very early age, as a separate individual, with a right to his own tastes and his own feelings will have a better chance of being in their turn respected by the grown child than does the parent who gives lavish presents but will not listen when the child tries to put forward his own, unfamiliar, often unwelcome point of view. To discipline a child means, for me, to teach him how to live with others – in the first place with ourselves. It does not mean 'breaking his spirit' so that he does not dare to disagree, but teaching him, not by precept but by our own attitudes towards him and towards others, that it is possible, indeed essential to disagree, but that this need not involve a loss of dignity. I was told once, at midnight on a remote Cornish railway station, by another mother of small children waiting for the same train to take us back from holiday, that she had been impressed by the saying of a philosopher in ancient China – 'Never let a child lose face'. When I heard this, I was impressed too. It is very easy to shame a child; sometimes difficult, but more rewarding is to make him feel that he is worthy of the respect we demand for ourselves.

If we accept the argument for having rules, the question of enforcement must then arise. Rules are made, as they say, to be broken, but only if they have generally been kept. In most families this is achieved through bribes, ranging from the promise of extra sweets to the more sophisticated reward of gratitude and approval; threats of anything from the nursery smack to parental anger, even the docking of privileges or pocket money, and in 90 per cent of cases these are enough. It is important, though, that authority is consistent, that the threats are not recognized to be empty and that the bribes are punctually fulfilled. The parent must not promise more than he or she is prepared to do.

Children are not the only learners in the family situation; a mother quickly finds out that if she is to be able to keep her word, she must never either threaten or promise more than she can perform. 'If you're not a good boy I won't take you shopping this morning' is meaningless if Johnny knows that she has got to go to the Co-op and there is no one to leave him with at home. She will also find that a punishment set in the future will almost certainly hurt her as much as the child, since when the specified time comes she will probably no longer be angry enough to enforce it with any heart. And finally I would hope that the fashion for long and elaborate explanations and arguments might die out in favour of the quick smack, administered where it probably hurts least (on the bottom in case anyone is not sure) and immediately, before the situation has escalated into total war. Children are primarily physical, not intellectual creatures, and they understand anger and love expressed in the cuff and the hug far more easily than they do an even temporary withdrawal of love.

One last point. In *Seven Winters*, Elizabeth Bowen (1943) gives a charming description of her childhood in Dublin. She says of her mother:

> Her only child had been born after nine years of waiting – and even I was able to understand that she could not take me or her motherhood for granted. She was so much desolated that she unnerved me when anything went wrong between her and me. If my mother was a perfectionist, she had the kind of wisdom that goes with that make-up. She explained to me candidly that she kept a governess because she did not want to scold me herself. To have to keep saying 'Do this', 'Don't do that', and 'No' to me would have been, as she saw it, a peril to everything.

With all due respect to Miss Bowen, about whose private life I know nothing, though I am a great admirer of her writing, I think her mother was wrong. One of the most demanding tasks the growing child has to face is the reconciling of his love and his hate for the same person – usually his mother. Until he has come to terms with this, he cannot himself be whole. For Miss Bowen's sake, I cannot help hoping that her governess sometimes contrived to make herself lovable and that her mother occasionally displayed irritation or some other human trait. Because, as parents, we must have the confidence to take action which our offspring will sometimes dislike. It is only when we are unsure of our own capacity to arouse and to retain their respect and their love that we are too frightened to teach them the rules of the game.

11

References

BOWEN, E. (1943) *Seven Winters* London: Longman

FREUD, A. (1966) *Normality and Pathology in Childhood* London: Hogarth Press

John Watts

Tell me what to do and I'll do it

When a parent comes to me and says, 'What my boy needs is more discipline,' I think I know what is meant. He needs to be told more authoritatively by his teachers what we want him to do, but what he does not necessarily want to do, and then punished by enforced pain or inconvenience if he does not do it. In that way he will learn that life is more comfortable when conforming and unless he is very stubborn, he will submit and obey. This parent makes it sound very simple. All we need to do is to assert the authority vested in us as schoolmasters and literally master our pupils; if we fail to do that then we are not worthy of our title and a right soft lot into the bargain.

This worries me. It worries me because it all takes for granted a style of teaching and learning that may have had relevance in some other times and places, but no longer seems applicable today; it worries me because that phrase 'what we want' assumes a uniform code of values, which today, like Henry Reed's piling swivel, in our case we do not have; and it worries me because it renders discipline into something discrete and detached from learning, a prerequisite to study, rather than something subtly interfused with it and taking its colour from it, a sort of all-weather coat rather than a skin.

I want to argue that discipline, far from being a general condition registered only in quantity, takes its form from the nature of the work in hand, determining the kind of relationship arising between teacher and student. If this is so, then we must start with curriculum and the sort of learning that we want to take place. After that we must ask what is the appropriate discipline. For all too often what that parent's boy needs is not more discipline, but a more appropriate

13

discipline. It is not so much a question of getting him to behave before he can learn anything, as one of what kind of behaviour will enable him to learn within the aims of the curriculum.

Traditionally, curriculum aims have been centred around the transference, from the teacher to the pupil, of an accepted body of knowledge and an accepted set of values. Freire (1972) has aptly called this the 'banking' concept of education, the teacher making the 'deposits'. For this to work, two factors were essential; first, agreement among the learned as to what knowledge was necessary and what values were honoured, and second, a body of acceptable knowledge which was sufficiently compact and stable for a school teacher to possess it all. The smaller the school, the more any one teacher had to know and the more he was expected to embody the values he was instilling into his pupils. He had to be a paragon of virtue and also had to convince everyone 'that one small head' could carry all he knew. Of course, with a staff of many specialists, the body of knowledge could be carved up and parcelled out into less daunting portions. However, the principle remained, that what needed to be known was known, that teachers knew it and had to convey it to their pupils who did not.

Such a model of learning carried with it an appropriate system of discipline. It arises from the relationship between master and disciple dictated by the model. Knowledge is seen as something external to the student, not necessarily related to his interests or concerns, something to be handed on from the past to the future. Knowledge is useful in as much as it bestows power and also gives entrée to the places of power. Traditionally, the content of curriculum was not of much intrinsic use. (When it consisted mainly of Classics it enabled MPs to call out the completions to each other's Latin tags across the floor of the House.) And it is worth noting that today few parents or employers give a fig for the content of examination syllabuses, so long as they see the right number of good grades coming up.

If, then, the body of knowledge is seen by the pupils to have scant relevance to their existence, the teacher is forced to adopt a position of authority to show that he knows that what he is teaching is for their ultimate good. He cannot afford, qua subject teacher, to associate with the personal interests of his charges, except in so far as this will render the necessary knowledge more palatable. The Theory of

Pythagoras, of the enclitic-ne, are either fascinating in themselves, or are made relatively painless by a personable teacher, or are forced down by threats and punishment. By whatever means the knowledge is transferred, the teacher is inevitably in the position of power, knowing what is right, correcting his pupils when wrong. He is judged by his skill in bringing his charges up to the mark; they are judged by their capacity to echo him and approximate to him. The crucial factor therefore in such a dispensation is obedience.

The whole discipline of transfer rests on the authority of the teacher, and the submission of his pupils. The teacher must be an authority in his subject, but he must also be an authority in all matters of behaviour, since learning, in this model, is concerned with regulating mental behaviour so that it conforms with that of the teacher. From this follow the ritual controls of behaviour that serve also to convey a value system in such a way that it cannot be questioned or modified except by outright rebellion. Teachers are set apart by peculiar garbs of office, tend to be elevated at high tables, on platforms or the classroom dais, adopt forms of speech that elevate them in a Johnsonian way. ('You have just committed an error of abbreviation, James,' said my friend Jim's headmaster when he told him his name.) The teacher's status was conferred upon him from above, and he tried to live up to it; in turn, his pupils were expected to show him respect for what he embodied, by calling him 'Sir', by standing up when addressed by him, by agreeing with him. The worst crimes for a pupil were being dishonest or disrespectful, because they threatened the structure of authority, the structure upon which education depended.

For centuries it has been possible to operate with such a discipline because those two criteria held: the body of necessary knowledge was compact and the social values of society remained relatively fixed. Relatively fixed, because it is only necessary that changes have not distorted the value system of grandparents for the grandchildren to inherit them. This is enough to establish what Margaret Mead (1970) has identified as a 'postfigurative' culture, one in which the young could learn from the old. The young were not expected to diverge or to develop individuality, but to submit and conform. Not all teachers were quite so blatant as Keate, headmaster of Eton in Shelley's day, who exclaimed 'Love God, boys, or I'll flog you till you do', but you only need to read how John Wesley brought up his own family to see how crucial it was thought to break the will of a child, for the parent-teacher to dominate.

Some hanker after this past: many teach as if it still existed. But a discipline arising from such a static and circumscribed curriculum, which in turn can be valid only if it accords to the needs of a society with a uniform set of values, cannot be appropriate today. The essential conditions are altered. The body of knowledge is now too great for any one person to master, and the values operating within society are diverse. The growth of knowledge has been at such an accelerated rate that no specialist can claim any longer to keep up with all that is known in his subject now, let alone which of it is relevant to the coming decades when his pupils will be replacing him. He is even less able to predict what will be added to that knowledge, or more important still, what will be the problems to which the next generation will address itself. He cannot foretell what new subjects will emerge, or how his own will relate to them. He can only extrapolate tentatively from the present. This is, of course, a very unnerving situation, and I suspect that many teachers hold on to the old discipline, based on authority and obedience, because it somehow convinces them that the old static curriculum still holds good, and the world's rate of change can be denied. Canute learnt otherwise.

As with the transference of knowledge, so with the transference of values: the process is only effective where the culture is postfigurative, and where there is congruence of attitude between teacher and parent. The latter situation has prevailed in independent and grammar schools. The grammar schools have been particularly effective instruments of preparation for the middle class, selecting for intake principally pupils of middle class origin, along with those destined to move out of working class into middle class, often at the cost of alienation from the family. (The extent to which this process may remain a mystery to the very teachers who are its agents, may be seen in Nell Keddie's (1972) paper 'Knowledge and control in the classroom'.) This certainly does not hold true across the whole comprehensive spectrum, nor, increasingly, can that congruence of aims and values be relied upon even in selective schools.

In a comprehensive system there is unlikely to be a majority of pupils who have been brought up to value long-term goals and

16

deferred satisfactions. Yet it is the child with that expectation who will suffer tedious schooling because he and his parents appreciate its instrumental value in achieving qualification and status. Teachers sharing this outlook, tend still to equate this with intelligence. ('He understands me, therefore he must be bright.') Those for whom the long-term goal provides insufficient motivation are classed as thick. Where the value of deferred satisfaction is generally appreciated, the teacher may expect results in terms of examination success from a discipline based on sticks and carrots. He may also achieve such results by adopting an authoritarian attitude. After all, if parent, pupil and teacher agree that the point of it all is to get good examination results and a better job, then it does not much matter if little of it makes sense or seems relevant to the inner life of the pupil or the outer life of the world at large. If the school, as an institution, supports the teacher whose methods involve setting pupils in competition one against the others, punishing those who, inevitably, achieve lower than average results, by humiliations, by detentions, by pointless punitive paper-filling, by physical punishment and by arousal of guilt at letting down the class, the school, the family, all will be accepted by a large proportion who get there in the end and can say with gratitude it was only because their teachers drove them. Unfortunately, across the whole comprehensive range only a minority do 'get there' by this definition, with, say, two or three A levels. If by this form of discipline the majority do not get there, then either they are left burdened with the guilt of failure, after all that everybody has done for them, or they will have rejected a system of discipline that is seen to bear no relationship to their own aims and interests. Teachers in turn will have labelled this majority as unresponsive to academic discipline or lacking it up there, or more likely, both.

To complicate the issue for teachers attempting to impose an academic discipline, an increasing number of middle class pupils are questioning and rejecting the long-term goals set by their parents. They see the rate of change in society being so great that the future no longer offers the certainty of security in a respectable white-collar job that it may have done to the last two generations. We are at a point where school leavers who would qualify for university are opting out in increasing numbers. They also see that quite apart from the future, the present itself has undergone so many changes that the garments of a past morality no longer fit. They observe that the middle class values of thrift, stability, self-denial, permanence, respect for authority, are not the necessary attributes for success or survival. They see that change of occupation, dwelling-place, marriage-partner are not so disastrous in consequence as their parents were brought up to believe. They see this rate of change and know that survival will depend on flexibility, ingenuity and fearlessness in the face of the unknown. And so they reject, or more exactly perhaps, accept that we have passed out of, the postfigurative culture that relied on our elders knowing all the answers and receiving gratitude and respect for it. As this dawns on the young, so they challenge or ignore (even more vexing) the wisdom and advice of their parents and those teachers who can be identified with them by age or manner. Such respect as they get has to be acquired: it is no longer coming to them by right of status.

If the appropriate discipline arises from the curriculum, what then is an appropriate curriculum for today? Unless it is designed to prepare an élite, or principally to provide certification, it must arise from the needs of the comprehensive intake. If it is to have any bearing on reality, its content cannot rest on information found useful in the past, nor on an existing culture to be transmitted to the future. Which might seem to dispose of all that teachers have striven to do up to now!

It has become fashionable to define curriculum in terms of measurable objectives as alternatives to public examinations with questionable content. Given Bloom's (1956) vast taxonomy of educational objectives with its three domains of 'cognitive', 'affective' and 'psychomotor', teachers could work out a sort of do-it-yourself curriculum, much as one might build up a salad in a self-service natural food restaurant. For a full account of the fallibility of such an approach, one could read chapter 3 of Douglas Holly's (1971) *Society, Schools and Humanity*. Fundamentally, we would still have a curriculum validated by outcomes, only now in behaviourist terms. What is still lacking is a programme for learning based on an interaction of the pupil's inner concern with social reality. The validation of such a curriculum will be a long-term process because it will turn ultimately on the success with which school students can as adults enter into and affect the changes that will shape their lives.

Derek Morrell expressed this forcefully in a lecture on the concept of curriculum shortly before he died in 1969:

> It is increasingly seen that institutional authority is relative to changing social norms, and that the successful management of social change demands a body of citizens who can make responsible choices with less support than in the past from precedent, tradition and dogma.

The curriculum appropriate to these demands will swing the focus from what is learnt to how it is learnt, it will be built less around inherited school subjects and more around seminal concepts, it will require students to enquire and conclude rather than be told what is to be known, and it will stimulate collaborative rather than competitive learning.

At present it is not difficult to find examples in schools of curriculum developments along some or most of these lines, but nearly always the new notions of curriculum have outstripped the concept of discipline, so that these innovations are themselves handicapped by the requirements of an inappropriate discipline, either within the area of school where it is taking place, or more often as a conflict with the ethos of the school as a whole. For instance, integrated humanities based on small-group work has been introduced into the first three years of a school. Its success depends among other things on the development of cooperative enterprise. Yet each week, in morning assembly, prominence is given to the announcement of competitive house merit points awarded for individual achievement.

Inescapably, though in the teeth of conservative resistance, new curriculum entails changed relationships and changed forms of discipline. The teacher is no longer the main source of knowledge or, more to the point, not even the one who selects all the problems to be solved, but becomes the facilitator, the one who helps the pupils formulate their own problems and then provides not the answers but the techniques for problem-solving, the one who suggests a line of enquiry. (As a maths teacher might now say: 'You've just come up with a new way of describing a cube. Why not go on and investigate all the properties of a cube that you can discover?') He then no longer embodies the discipline of study, but is entering into that discipline with his students, so that they both submit to the requirements of study. The teacher is able to detail what must be done if the job is to be completed, whether it is checking the work of an experiment in physics or justifying a conclusion drawn in sociology, but the demands arise from the work in hand, for which the student must see the real point.

That is the discipline of motivated work, with the teacher interpreting the demands. Where the student is operating choice in the work undertaken, he needs to learn to respect the choices made by others. What he wants to do may be restricted by what others want to do. Thus he needs to learn respect for a corporate authority and accept the social disciplines that render collaboration practical. So it does not become a matter of each individual doing what he likes, when and if he likes, but rather of working out, and where necessary enforcing, the mutual accommodations of a community. Students whose study increasingly entails enquiry, autonomous work programmes, conclusions open to rational verification, creations unique to their makers, will not blindly accept a discipline of controls imposed impersonally and unquestionably from above. And teachers who in the workshop or laboratory say 'Let's examine this problem together and see what ways of tackling it we can devise between us,' cannot in all conscience turn round and say 'But here in school we have this social problem: it will be solved by your obeying the following rules.' Once a collaborative approach has been adopted over curriculum problems, so it will spread into the social life of a school. Which teachers may either dread or welcome. But they certainly cannot have it both ways, enquiry plus enterprise in class, but unquestioning obedience outside it.

At Countesthorpe we have tried to take these arguments to their logical and practical conclusions. I would claim that all our innovations spring from the curriculum offered and the style of discipline emerging is the outcome of it. The main innovatory features are seen in our architecture, our style of study based on small groups and individual work with an appropriate style of staff-student relationship, our involvement with the local public as a community college, and our system of participatory internal government. From the start staff agreed to avoid conventional ritual means of declaring teacher authority: there was no required dress, no given regulations other than a refusal to tolerate antisocial behaviour, no exclusion of pupils from areas used by staff or from meetings. Every effort was made to create that 'reciprocity of feeling and aspiration' between staff and student, pleaded for by Derek Morrell. First names are an accepted form of address and staff are available pretty continuously. (Once you abandon ritual exchanges, the onus lies on expressive ones, which means incessant dialogue between staff and students.) All very wearing! And at first it was undoubtedly intoxicating for some students and alarming for many parents and administrators. To complete the structure of corporate rather than hierarchical authority, the headmaster, though having as good a voice as anyone else in the government, does not exercise a veto but accepts the corporate decisions on policy. The final appeal on any decision is settled by the Moot, our collegiate body of staff and students.

Thus the discipline is of a completely different nature from that experienced by parents and other local adults when they were at school. For some it is incomprehensible that any discipline can exist at all if it does not stem from the head's authority, by hierarchical command down through his staff and prefects, enforced by rules, punishments and the rituals of domination from canes, formal address, and morning assembly for moral harangues. Some having argued thus, do not need to know any more: indiscipline *must* be rife and there will always be evidence for it! Witness, pupils wandering out of school during hours asking impertinent questions under the guise of conducting enquiries, pupils pushing past visitors in corridors as if they owned the place instead of showing appreciation for all the privileges conferred upon them, pupils wasting time chattering or playing cards during lesson times.

And yet ... and yet they are learning. Visitors who actually listen to the pupils regularly report how refreshingly they will explain what they are doing and why they are doing it. Kids who were previously school-phobics now attend regularly, even if they do not always seem to be doing much. Parents, even some deeply suspicious ones, report that their children like the school, thereby further deepening the suspicion as often as not. And, to pick out one more factor from a host of others, teachers who had begun to despair of schools as institutions, resentful of petty restrictions and uninvited conflicts, find the chance of relationships that enable learning to occur without warping their own natures. I said to one young teacher provocatively, 'But we produce problems of our own even in ridding ourselves of so many conventional ones, don't we?' 'Sure we face problems, but they are the real ones,' he replied.

What did he mean by real problems? Well, we have lost some of the self-imposed problems, like how to enforce an unwanted uniform or hair length, how to administer someone else's retributive punishments, how to interpret rules laid down by someone else's authority. But we face new ones. For instance, how convincingly to answer demands from the old world that we stick to 'the tried methods'; how to devise resource material in sufficient quantities and make their retrieval easy; how to avoid the pupils' friendship groupings from so dominating the study situation that they fail to learn how to negotiate and collaborate with workmates not of their own choosing; how to accept that whatever new ethos the school may have created, Old Adam is still on the register somewhere, resents compulsory education, and in an open school will need curbing if he is not to distract those who on balance see some advantages in being here.

It is a discipline in which roles have changed for both pupils and teachers, not suddenly and not too easily, but by being grown into. For both, there exist pressures to keep pushing them back into the old familiar roles, for the pupil to remain helpless and for the teacher to dominate. One needs reminders such as that given by David Cooper (1967) when describing his community innovation Villa 21 in *Psychiatry and Antipsychiatry*: 'Perhaps the most central characteristic of authentic leadership is the relinquishing of the impulse to dominate others.' For the teacher the most difficult accomplishment is to know how to exert pressure without domination. He has an obligation as a teacher to make demands, but as Richard Jones (1968) has made so clear in *Fantasy and Feeling in Education*, those demands ('threats' he even calls them) need to follow upon the pupil's achievement of security within the community and competence in tackling his work. Given those conditions creative learning occurs. With no sense of community, but only of aloneness coupled with helplessness, a student will move towards neurotic breakdown when faced with threatening demands. And neurosis is the commonest cause of failure in our time.

So we are forging out a new discipline that is appropriate to a significant curriculum. The discipline is one which requires the teacher to make demands without dominating, but which also requires him to maximize the possibility of community and competence, and requires of the student that he accepts responsibility for his development towards autonomy. This discipline is attuned to a relevant curriculum because it applies not to that postfigurative culture that we must realize is vanished, but to the emergent prefigurative culture in which the old will have to learn from the young. To conclude with Margaret Mead: 'We must create new models for adults who can teach their children not what to learn, but how to learn and not what they should be committed to, but the value of commitment.'

References
BERNSTEIN, B. (1967) Open schools, open society? *New Society* 14th September
BLOOM, B. S. *et al* (1956) *Taxonomy of Educational Objectives* London: Longman
COOPER, D. (1967) *Psychiatry and Antipsychiatry* London: Tavistock
FREIRE, P. (1972) *Pedagogy of the Oppressed* Harmondsworth: Penguin
HOLLY, D. (1971) *Society, Schools and Humanity* London: MacGibbon and Kee
JONES, R. M. (1968) *Fantasy and Feeling in Education* New York: New York University Press; London: ULP; Harmondsworth: Penguin
KEDDIE, N. (1972) 'Knowledge and control in the classroom' in Michael Young (ed) *Knowledge and Control: New Directions in the Sociology of Education* London: Collier-Macmillan
MEAD, M. (1970) *Culture and Commitment* London: Bodley Head
MORRELL, D. (1969) Happiness is not a meal ticket *Times Educational Supplement* 19th December
WATTS, J. (1971) Community school *Times Educational Supplement* 23rd April
WATTS, J. (1972) Looking forward and looking back *Ideas* October

Robert Brooks

The right relationship

It is an oversimplification to state that schools are places in which education occurs, for the diversity of location, social environment, facilities, staff attitudes, overall ethos and sense of community invariably means that whilst schools may be broadly recognized as having educational functions, the concept of education and its practice vary greatly from school to school. It is always more appropriate, therefore, to discuss the problems of discipline in *education* rather than discipline in *schools*. The former ought to have a measure of universal significance whilst the latter will be strongly conditioned by local or parochial influences as well as by the personal aspirations and prejudices of the people who form the individual schools.

Nor is it sufficient to accept without definition what is meant by the term *discipline* which is often used synonymously with the term *order* whilst at other times it is used professionally to refer to the body of information and the approaches essential to the study of a particular subject area. No one can deny that some basic or minimal code of rules are in man's best interests. Man and his environment being what they are, some basic rules are imperative for any form of social life and these rules will and do create obligations but such that will vary from society to society and group to group. The dangers inherent in confusing the terms *order* and *discipline* lie in the fact that acquiescence to rules may too readily be regarded as indicative of social adjustment or the achievement of integrated personal learning. Whilst the ability to accept certain rules may be a mark of social maturity, this is not always or necessarily so. Subservience to rules may be brought about by threat, coercion and fear. Where this is so, obedience may well be no more than the overt expression of frustration and overanxiety.

Within any community – and every school should have the quality of community – some rules are necessary but only those are justified which serve to establish a pattern of order through which it is possible for the people within it to relate to each other. The rules adopted in a school or classroom should be such that they facilitate the teacher in identifying and relating to every child whilst still retaining the sense of group life which can be a vitalizing influence in any classroom or learning situation. Rules for their own sake have no creative quality and their only justification lies in the extent to which they contribute to the development of the authenticity of the community they are devised to serve and to the fulfilment of those who form the community.

Attempts to define what is to be understood by the term *order* in the context of education are fraught with difficulty for attitudes to *order* and ideas about the rules which are necessary to bring about the sort of pupil behaviour which is considered desirable are conditioned by the attitudes of teachers and others involved in school administration. Teachers perceive their role in many ways. There are those who believe their function is simply the transmission of information within their given discipline whilst others view their role in a wider context embracing the total development of the child as a person. Then there are many teachers who view their function and that of the school to be such that the sort of classroom order they require from children intrudes upon areas of behaviour peripheral to or even having no part of the disciplined learning which they seek to promote. The children's personal conduct, taste and social conventions are often regulated as part of their school life to such an extent that apparent learning difficulties are caused which, on investigation, may be found to have nothing specifically to do with the material of a subject discipline itself but are brought about by the damage which such intrusions can cause to the empathetic rapport which must exist between teachers and pupils as persons if effective and integrated learning is to occur.

Because it is necessary for there to be some degree of order in an effective learning situation, there is a tendency to argue that concepts such as authority, freedom, punishment, sanctions and the like form an integral part of the learning process. Although these concepts have a relevance to learning processes, no teacher should find it necessary to preface his teaching by psychological threat or any other form of coercion. The child should not be made to feel that the beginning of each day or lesson in school represents a confrontation in which the teacher's 'armour' is superior. Instead he should have, as a first awareness, a sense of welcome which will stimulate an attitude of hospitality to new experience. But even the most competent teacher who has great empathetic insight will come across children who will not or who are unable to accept the order which is an essential prerequisite to the discipline of the learning situation. Such children not only threaten the effective learning of the rest of the group or class but may also cause the teacher to feel threatened in some way. Such situations can be exacerbated by the sheer weight of numbers of children. Next to the consideration of the quality of the teacher as a person, perhaps the most important factor in the quality of the life of a school is the teacher/pupil ratio. Overlarge classes can have the effect of causing some pupils to be overtly disruptive in order to establish an acknowledgment of their identity or may lead teachers into making their approach exclusively to the group as a whole, thereby removing the possibility of establishing personal relationships. Many such teachers feel compelled to enter the classroom with one priority, that of gaining *control over* the children. Whilst this is understandable, it must also be regarded as one of the principal causes of the violence, disruptive behaviour and low levels of attainment for which many schools are, from time to time, criticized. Classes and groups must be of such a size that both the children and the teachers can feel the relationships which are essential to human growth and personal development.

Education is concerned with development and growth. We nourish in order to stimulate towards further growth and the quality of the nourishment offered to children by our educational services should be such that every aspect of each child's being is stimulated and nurtured. The extent to which the child feels himself being treated with respect as an authentic person will condition the degree of ease which he feels within himself. The child who senses himself being fulfilled by learning situations which minister to his growth will not create behavioural problems for the teacher. Any breakdown of classroom *order* must be regarded as evidence of unease amongst the pupils and it is no solution to repress disorder or to react with punitive responses. Of course there are many who will contradict this view and maintain that once a teacher has 'got control' over his pupils, order will prevail. But sanctions, rewards and punishments tend to act upon the child externally and because this is so they tend to achieve, at best, only a measure of external or apparent conformity. And it has been amply demonstrated in many schools that this sort of conformity is short-lived and produces a more disturbing degree of reactive violence later on.

The sort of order which is a prerequisite for learning at depth is an order which finds a response within the child. It is true that sanctions, rewards and punishments (to say nothing of acts of spite or revenge) will be psychologically and emotionally interpreted by the child and will, therefore, affect the inner persona but such devices do not create the essential link between the teacher as a person of empathy and the child as a person striving for growth and authenticity. The effective teacher is the one who knows as much as possible *about* the children he teaches but who carries that knowledge into a dimension of understanding which enables him to establish with every child a degree of reciprocity of feeling which is really empathetic.

The good teacher is 'first and foremost *a person* and this fact is the most important and determining thing about him' (Combs 1965). The good teacher is the one who is able to assist his pupils in their search for effective ways of satisfying their urge for growth and for coming to terms with the world in which they live. The teacher's function – and I prefer the term *function* to the term *role* – is to contribute to the authentic self-realization of every pupil. He should stimulate children to question and reflect upon the meaningfulness of the learning situations and informational resources offered to them. It is only through this thoughtful and reflective process that children can come to have an awareness of those things which have personal significance. Linear timetabling and rigidity in the sequential treatment of subject matter ought not to be overstressed and children must be brought to realize that a mistake is not some form of minor 'crime' which merits some punitive reaction. Mistakes can be creative in the sense that they can lead to new insights, the development of more realistic goals and valid personal growth. The teacher who is

C

affronted by mistakes is not likely to be competent to create a learning environment which has personal relevance for the children.

Yet for many schools and teachers, the term *discipline* carries the connotation of the student conforming: of not making academic, technical or social mistakes. In such an atmosphere, integrated learning cannot occur for the pupil will feel under threat and this will give rise to an intolerable level of anxiety which will cause the child to shut himself up in defence rather than opening himself up to experience. The only form of discipline which is lasting, effective and creative is that which stems from within the person. Externally devised structures, routines and 'traditions' only serve to take away from the growing child the sense of choice. And it is only when the child becomes aware that he has choice that he begins to know that he has a responsibility for himself. Once a child is aware of that sort of responsibility, he is on the road to self-actualization.

All this is not to say that roles have no place in education, but it does mean that they are or ought to be temporary things which are only purposeful in a wider and deeper context. The dangers of roles arise when they are given an indelibility which limits the freedom of the person. Roles are only safe when they serve but do not dominate relationships. They are only justifiable when they can be easily set aside. All too often, teachers confine themselves to being role players who appear hell-bent on trying to get children to give up satisfactions. The teacher's relationship with children ought to be freeing and non-threatening so that they can consider their choices with greater discipline and choose those which offer them the deepest sense of 'becoming persons'.

Every child is either becoming or diminishing as a person. The talents, feelings and skills of many children atrophy and die under the judgmental gaze of the teacher. Confidence and aspiration are destroyed and replaced by fear associated with apathy. The dreams and hopes of the becoming organism are stifled and the creative fun is taken away from learning and life. Creativity is too often viewed as a lesser goal than grammatical conformity or technical correctness so that the child is often denied the initial use of lucid but informal modes of communicating. On the other hand, there are those teachers who, by their personal charismatic qualities invite children to grow along with them — transmitting to them a sense of confidence and urging them to nurture and fulfil all that they are or may become, These are those whose teaching stems from their inner resources as persons and who are free to communicate and relate to the inner being of the children as persons. Such teachers are able to share the delights, hopes, fears and joys of those they teach while their feeling of sharing is felt by the children to be authentic so that they are enabled to live more deeply and fully. These are the teachers who teach with enthusiasm in its real sense, from the 'god within' to the 'god within'.

Schools, and more particularly classrooms, can be one of two things. They can represent to children either enclosing walls which frustrate their realization as persons or be centres and focal points from which both inner and outer worlds of experience are revealed. They can be places of containment and restriction or they can have the ethos of nourishment and ongoing stimulation. If they are perceived by children as the former, then they will try to evade the censorship of their behavioural patterns and there will be a breakdown in the order essential to effective learning. Coercive frustration is an ineffective aid to learning just as is the laissez-faire permissiveness which has sometimes been incorrectly perceived as being child-centred education.

In work carried out at schools such as Summerhill (Neill 1962) and Kneesworth (Brooks 1972) and at the therapeutic community at Finchden Manor (Burn 1956, Lyward 1969) an essential prerequisite is that the uniqueness of each child is recognized and respected. It has never been sufficient for those who have been involved in such communities to regard the young people who come to them as being 'deviant' or 'difficult'. They are persons. Their behavioural patterns may deviate from the norms which society finds necessary or acceptable, but that can never be a justification for denying any child his integrity as a person.

Our experience at Kneesworth Hall School showed that behavioural adjustments came about as a subsequent reaction by a boy to an inner feeling that he was not being judged and condemned but was being accepted as a person, being endowed with choice and, therefore, faced with responsibility for himself. The choices which those boys and, indeed, which any person has to make are painful and, at times, nearly intolerable but it is only when children can be given the experience of choice that they are drawn to face the pain of responsibility.

The work which was attempted at Kneesworth Hall School rested upon what appeared to many to be a contradictory philosophy. Boys who had been compelled by society to come to the school expected to find their personal privacy invaded and to be compelled to conform to some externally devised routine which would act as some sort of yardstick against which their social progress could be measured. And yet, on arrival, they found that their freedom was restored to them so that each stayed by his own decision. The boys were not subjected to threat enforced demands for conformity but rather, they were exposed to that sort of freedom which is both painful and demanding. We did not usurp their personalities nor did we accept the transfer on to us of all their decision-making.

It was our experience at Kneesworth Hall School that until the boys faced the pain of responsibility, they could not move towards becoming their own authentic and unique selves. No teacher should regard it as his function to remove from the child those choices which breed responsibility, even though there is a degree of pain involved in decision-making. It is when the teacher usurps the child's decision-making responsibility that the child is deprived of the feeling of purpose. The child who lacks the sense of purpose becomes apathetic and the apathetic child is the child who readily disrupts the learning processes.

Buber (1947) defines man as a creature capable of entering into living relationships. In personal relationships – and this is the medium of true education – one life opens up to another so that one person experiences the mystery of the other through the mystery of one's self. Two people participate in each other's lives not merely in some corporeal way but ontologically. This quality of relationship must not be confused with the concept of solicitude proposed by Heideggar which has about it the offering of assistance – of *doing good*. Buber pleads for relationships in which the inner life of the one is set in a direct and empathetic relationship with another. The teacher must strive for the quality of relationships with those he teaches which will enable him to echo Buber's (1958) words: 'Not only do I accept the other as he is, but I confirm him in myself, and then in him, in relation to his potentiality that is meant by him and that it can now be developed, it can evolve – it can answer the reality of life.' For this is the need for any person – to try to answer the reality of life without denying its mystery.

But the 'I – Thou' of Buber must never be exploited without the recognition of his 'I – It'. The uniqueness of every child must be respected. The teacher must perceive what qualities lie within each child and allow them to be and to grow. The teacher's injunction to a child to come alive is an invitation for the child to grow and become the unique self latent within the inner fastnesses of his being. But the teacher who is able and willing to communicate this wish for authentic growth must not shrink from realizing and communicating his awareness that there is, in growth towards becoming, a great deal of pain. There are demands to be met and hurts to be sustained and obstacles to be overcome and burdens to be borne. There also has to to be the acceptance of the sort of pain which comes from our never knowing all the answers. In fact, living involves us in a mystery in which the questions we ask ourselves are more vital than the few answers we may elucidate. It is in the questions that lie the thrill of learning. Most, if not all the thrill is lost when we have found or devised an answer. It is vital that those who teach should recognize this. All too often the child who poses a question is accused of digressing or laying red herrings. To deviate from the rigid structure of the curriculum is not to invite disorder. It is more likely to be true that to frustrate the questioning child is to bring about boredom and consequent disorder, both within the child and the group.

Our present society is one in which children are in great peril. There is violence and deception all around. Yet there are also great opportunities which give reasonable hope for real living. Provided we do not react against a young and questioning generation by coldness in attitude and punitive devices, then there is a chance that we can avoid producing a deeply hurt generation.

People live when they are free to be true to those qualities which they feel within themselves and when their living can be authentic to those qualities. We live when we love. When we are involved in but not usurping the lives of others and when we are committed within our inner selves to creating, wondering and suffering. But love cannot thrive within the prison of the selfish person. Love only grows and renews itself when it offers itself. The key word here is *offer* for we must, if we will love, offer our loving and accept the vulnerability of its rejection. It is not enough for the teacher to engage in associative relationships. The medium through which the teacher meets the children must not be confined by the associations which emanate from the curriculum and timetable. These should serve and not dominate the relationships which can make the school a living and learning community. The only sort of teacher/pupil relationships which will foster real, effective and integrated learning are those which have loving as their model. And the essence of loving relationships is not to be found in linear concepts but in the depth of shared experience.

My own plea, therefore, is not for the adoption of some sort of permissive progressiveness in our schools but that those who administer or teach in schools shall take a close look at the needs of the children whose right it is that they shall be nourished in every way appropriate to them as potentially unique persons. This involves every teacher coming to as great an awareness of himself as possible. Authoritarianism in schools is an attitude which stems from fear, the fear of the teacher to know himself so that he sees any deviation from his own set objectives as something which threatens him and from which he must defend himself. The teacher needs to be as open to his own experience as should the children who form his classes. In such a democratic atmosphere, where there is real interrelation at depth, children will come not merely to maintain some form of status quo both within themselves and society but will, through their own enrichment as persons, enrich the community which is our society.

References

BUBER, M. (1947) *Between Man and Man* London: Routledge and Kegan Paul

BUBER, M. (1958) *I and Thou* Edinburgh: T. and T. Clark

BROOKS, R. (1972) *Bright Delinquents: The Story of a Unique School* Windsor: NFER

BURN, M. (1956) *Mr Lyward's Answer* London: Hamish Hamilton

COMBS, A. W. (1965) *The Professional Education of Teachers: A Perceptual View of Teacher Preparation* Boston: Allyn and Bacon

LYWARD, G. L. (1969) 'The school as a therapeutic community' in S. H. Foulkes and G. Stewart Prince (eds) *Psychiatry in a Changing Society* London: Tavistock

NEILL, A. S. (1962) *Summerhill* London: Gollancz; Harmondsworth: Penguin

Derek Wright

The punishment of children

It is probable that most teachers and parents regard punishing children as a necessary if regrettable part of the process of bringing them up to be social beings. The intention behind it is to stop them behaving in undesirable ways and to train them in self-control so that they can be relied upon to behave appropriately when they are not being directly supervised. We punish children in order that punishment may become unnecessary.

In practice, of course, it frequently fails to produce the results we want and often has consequences we do not want. It is observable that some children's behaviour deteriorates steadily the more frequently and intensely they are punished. Observations of this kind, together with a natural revulsion against the idea of punishment, have led many people to argue that it has no role at all in the sane and healthy upbringing of children. Advocates of this view have sometimes cited in its defence some of the earlier psychological experiments on the effects of punishment on human and animal subjects; experiments conducted mostly between the years 1930 to 1950. These experiments seemed to show that the effects of punishment are transitory, that they are weaker than the effects of positive reward, and that they can all too easily produce neurotic and maladaptive behaviour. In general the results seemed to support the educational doctrine that the best policy in child rearing is to ignore undesirable responses and to positively reward desirable behaviour that is incompatible with them.

Until recently this doctrine was widely accepted by many child psychologists and little further research was done into the matter, though the study of the effects of punishment on animals has continued (Church 1963 and Solomon 1964). In the last decade, however, interest in the subject has revived. This has been due to the recognition both that many of the early studies suffered from serious weaknesses in design, and also that the question is not whether in some general sense punishment is effective but how and under what conditions it has particular sorts of effect. This recent research, though it is far from answering all the questions we might ask, does suggest that punishment has a useful role in the development of self-control in children. It is this recent experimentation which will be reviewed here.

At this juncture it is necessary to say something about what is meant by punishment. It is notoriously difficult to arrive at a precise definition which escapes being in some measure tautological; for punishment has to be defined in terms of its effects upon the individual, and it is these very effects which we wish to leave open for investigation. For our present purposes, however, precision is not so important, and what follows is intended only as a loose and preliminary statement.

It is useful, initially, to distinguish 'negative reinforcement' in general from 'punishment' as one of its more limited forms. By negative reinforcement we shall mean, roughly, any action by one person which has unpleasant emotional consequences for another and which the other is thereby motivated to avoid in the future. For convenience the unpleasant emotional response will be labelled anxiety, though many other labels, such as fear, pain, embarrassment, discomfort and disappointment, may on occasion be more appropriate. At a relatively trivial level negative reinforcement is likely to be a feature of all social interaction, and is virtually unavoidable. For example, forgetting someone's name or ceasing to attend closely to what he is saying can both function as negative reinforcers. We can then reserve the word punishment for negatively reinforcing acts which are more or less intentional and deliberate. The more professional we are as educators the more our actions should be lifted to the level of intentionality. So, deliberately ignoring a child's behaviour can sometimes be as much a punishment as direct verbal reproof.

There is evidence which at first sight might appear to put this simple definition in question. For example: animal experimentation has shown that punishment can sometimes actually increase the likelihood of a response occurring, and it is quite a common observation that people may positively seek to be punished. However, what such observations show, is that punishment can have effects in addition to anxiety. For instance, it may, through conditioning, have come to signal the occurrence of some desirable event such as the cessation of guilt or the fact that others are paying attention. Under some circumstances (perhaps all) it may evoke anger and hostility, a point to which we shall return later.

It is important to stress that the 'experimental' study of punishment constitutes only a small part of the total evidence available. Most existing data come from field studies using a correlational design. For example, it has been consistently found that the high use of physical punishment in the home by parents is associated with high levels of aggression in their children outside the home (see Becker 1964). But data of this kind does not allow us to infer the direction of causation. Does the aggression cause the punishment, the punishment the aggression, or both? Only the experimental design allows us to sort this out. In the typical experiment the experimenter himself arranges for the subjects to be punished. He is then able to vary systematically one or more aspects of the punishing process and observe its effects on behaviour under conditions in which all other relevant factors are held constant or randomized. If the experiment is done well it is possible to conclude with some confidence whether or not differences in punishment procedures are causally related to differences in self-control.

In most experiments the punishments used have been a loud noise, verbal reproof (such as 'No, you musn't touch that!') or taking back sweets previously given to the child. Forbidden acts have included breaking a simple rule or playing with an attractive toy. In testing for the effects of punishment the child is normally left alone in a situation in which he is tempted to do the forbidden thing but in which, unknown to him, the experimenter can observe what he does.

But from the teacher's point of view there are certain obvious limitations to the value of such research. In the first place it is always slow and piecemeal. Only one or two aspects of punishment can be isolated and studied at a time, and the number waiting to be studied is considerable. Once these aspects have been studied in isolation then they must be examined in combination to see how they interact with each other. Since it is quite common for later research to lead to a revaluation of earlier work, there is the constant danger that educational policies will be prematurely influenced by results. Then for ethical reasons it is only possible to use very attenuated forms of punishment in the experimental situation. Most experiments have so far been performed only on young children, and the number that can be studied in any one experiment is always small. The controlled experiment always entails taking the phenomenon to be studied out of its normal context. All these, and other, considerations emphasize the need for caution in generalizing results to 'real life' situations. But the fact remains that the experiment is uniquely able to establish the existence of causal relationships; and when taken in conjunction with field studies of a correlational kind and everyday experience it does have a contribution to make to the formulation of educational policies.

In daily life the time interval between committing a forbidden act and being punished for it may vary widely. In a much quoted experiment on puppies, Solomon *et al* (1968) demonstrated that animals punished just before eating forbidden food held out longer against the temptation to eat it than others who had been punished after eating it for a minute or so. Several experiments (for example, Aronfreed and Reber 1965, and Walters *et al* 1965) have shown that the same effect of timing holds true with children also. The children were reprimanded either just before touching a certain toy or at intervals up to thirty seconds after they had touched it. Resistance to the temptation to touch the toy when left alone with it afterwards declined as the time interval increased. Though other experiments have not succeeded in demonstrating the effect clearly, and though timing interacts with other factors in the situation, it can be said that, other things being equal, the closer the punishment is to the moment the act is about to be performed the more effective it is in inhibiting the act.

The explanation of this finding most often advanced (for example, by Aronfreed 1968) is that when the child is punished, anxiety in its strongest form is conditioned to the other factors present at the time. If these include the intention to do the act and all the preparatory actions of doing it, then this strong anxiety will be evoked just prior to the act and serve as a barrier to doing it. If punishment follows the act it will associate anxiety in its strongest form with those factors present after the act has been performed; and though the anxiety will so to speak spread back to its beginning, it will then be in a weaker form. However useful this explanation is it is probably not the whole story. Experiments reported by Cheyne and Walters (1970), in which physiological measures were taken of anxiety level during punishment, indicate that a given sanction is more anxiety arousing when it interrupts an ongoing action than when it follows it. The timing effect may therefore be due to differences in the intensity of the punishment effect rather than to the timing itself.

Experimental findings tend to support the popular view that, other things being equal, the more severe the punishment the greater its inhibiting effect. But other things seldom are equal, and there are at least two important qualifications to be made. The first is well brought out in an experiment by Aronfreed (1968) and Leff. Children had to learn by being punished to discriminate between two toys, one of which they could play with, the other not. When the discrimination was made easy because the toys were very different, self-control in the testing situation was better when the punishment used was relatively intense. However, when the discrimination was difficult because the toys differed only in subtle ways, the relatively less severe punishment resulted in more self-control. In this experiment children had to learn to distinguish the toys as well as to resist the temptation to play with one of them. It is therefore somewhat closer to ordinary moral training where we frequently expect children to learn quite complicated and subtle discriminations. What this experiment shows is that if we want children to learn something complex, we are likely to defeat our own ends if we punish the child so much that he becomes too aroused for effective learning. The second qualification is that relatively severe forms of punishment appear to have undesirable side-effects. Of course these have not been investigated experimentally on human subjects; but numerous observations indicate that it can lead to neurotic symptoms, chronic anxiety, deep resentment towards the punishing agent, and a strong motive to avoid being found out. These considerations underline the value of keeping the intensity of punishment down to the minimal level.

In the administration of sanctions, teachers and others in positions of authority in institutions, cannot be guided solely by their influence upon the individual but also by their influence on others who know about the matter. Headmasters commonly feel that they must 'make an example' of an offender so that others will be deterred from misbehaving as well. A number of experiments (for example, Walters *et al* 1963, 1965 and Walters and Parke 1964) show that there is some validity in the assumption that children are deterred by watching others being punished. In these experiments children watched a film in which another child played with a forbidden toy. In one condition an adult appeared and rewarded the child, in another he punished the child, and in a third condition no adult appeared at all. Those who saw the child punished were distinctly more inhibited about touching the toy when subsequently left alone with it. Moreover, variations in the timing of the punishment of the model were reflected in the varying strengths of the observers' resistance to temptation.

There is now a considerable body of data on the nature of imitation in children. It is clear that watching another child breaking a rule and getting away with it has a powerful disinhibitory effect upon the observer. If the model is punished, this disinhibitory influence is neutralized. However, what is not clear yet is whether vicarious punishment can have as inhibiting an effect as direct punishment, and such evidence as there is suggests that it does not. Furthermore it may be expected that the relationship the observer has with the model and with the punishing agent will have an important bearing upon the effectiveness of vicarious punishment, not to mention the perceived justice of the punishment, and these are aspects of the problem that do not yet appear to have been studied.

When an adult punishes a child it is reasonable to expect both that the prior relationship between them will influence the effectiveness of the punishment and that the act of punishing will in turn have consequences for the relationship. Very little is known about the latter and so far no attempts to study it experimentally have been made. We may presume that the effect of the punishment will be negative. However, an experiment on puppies by Fisher (reported in Cheyne and Walters 1970) raises the possibility that it may not be as simple as that. In this experiment it was found that puppies who had been both rewarded and punished by the experimenter became more closely attached to him than puppies who had only been rewarded. It is possible therefore that under certain circumstances punishment may strengthen relationships. There is some evidence that in very young children strong attachment and strong aggression towards mother tend to go together. Nevertheless, because punishment is likely to evoke hostility towards the punisher and to result in the conditioning of anxiety to him, we can reasonably expect that the effect of punishment will usually be to erode or disrupt relationships, and it is probably wise for teachers and parents to do some discreet repair work after they have had to administer sanctions.

There is much more evidence available on the way the prior relationship between adult and child qualifies the sanctioning effect. Field studies point firmly to the conclusion that close attachment to one or two adults during the first years of life greatly facilitates the development of self-control, and it can be argued that without such attachment conscience is inevitably stunted. The mechanism of 'identification' is usually invoked to explain this. The notion is complex but the basic idea is that through attachment the child's idea of the adult enters in some degree into his definition of himself, and hence blame by the adult becomes self-blame. The child is on the side of the punishing agent, at least partly, and thereby comes to adopt his attitudes towards himself. Without such attachment the child may well learn to be prudent in avoiding punishment but he is unlikely to acquire the capacity to resist the temptation to misbehave when the chance of being found out looks slim.

The experimental control of attachment is hardly practicable except in its most attenuated forms, but it can be argued that if its effect is detectable under those conditions we may be even more confident of its importance in its stronger forms. The usual procedure is well illustrated in an experiment by Parke and Walters (1967). They manipulated the attachment variable by having the experimenter interact with the children in a warm and friendly fashion for a total of some forty minutes, and compared the effects of subsequent punishment by him with a control condition in which the experimenter was present with the children for the same amount of time but remained cool and detached. The results showed that even this transient and shallow degree of relationship clearly increased the effectiveness of punishment in inducing behavioural inhibitions.

Other experiments have demonstrated the converse of this, that the value of praise is enhanced if the child is first deprived of it for a short time. But whatever the explanation we prefer, there seems little doubt that both at a relatively superficial level and also in a more

39

committed and long lasting sense, when the child likes the punishing agent the probability that punishment for misbehaviour will result in later self-control is much increased. Whatever short-term benefits it may have, a discipline based on fear and the assertion of power is not the most appropriate if we wish to encourage the development of the child's conscience.

One of the most important aspects of the punishing situation is the nature and extent of the talk the adult engages in. This talk can serve a number of functions. It can be the mode of punishment through expressions of displeasure and the use of such evaluative terms as 'bad', 'naughty', and so on. Then it helps to draw the child's attention to those features of the situation we want him to think about, and it can give him information about the effects of his action on others. But perhaps its most significant function is that it can help the child to construe his actions in a certain way, to structure them cognitively and to relate them to general rules. The purpose of punishing a child for stealing from the larder is not just to stop him stealing from the larder but to stop him stealing in any context. For this to happen the inhibiting anxiety must be associated with the general concept of 'me stealing', and the child has to be taught how to apply the concept of stealing to his own behaviour in a wide variety of situations.

In justifying his punishment to the child there are broadly three kinds of explanatory talk the adult can engage in. He can focus upon the wickedness of the child, contenting himself with saying what a naughty and unpleasant boy he is. If this is repeatedly done and is not balanced by more positive evaluations on other occasions, the child is likely in the end simply to accept that he is a bad person and that there is little he can do about it. There is experimental evidence that when self-esteem is damaged moral controls are lowered as well (Aronson and Mettee 1968). Secondly, the adult may concentrate upon the offence in relation to himself, upon the way the child's action has upset and disappointed him and upon the implied affront to his authority. When every offence on the child's part, whether it directly concerns the adult or not, is interpreted by him as constituting disobedience of him, then the child is likely to construe all moral issues in terms of obedience to authority. There is ground for thinking that this may retard his full moral development by preventing him from achieving moral autonomy and from becoming himself a source of moral evaluation. Thirdly, the adult can emphasize the general nature of the offence, giving reasons for judging it wrong, explaining its effect upon others, and relating it to future occasions. When this is consistently done the child is given the necessary criteria for making judgments of his own, and to some extent anyway the wrongness of the act is dissociated from the authority of the adult. Explanatory talk of this kind is unlikely to be accompanied by severe punishment, since it presupposes an adult who is fairly cool and reasonable. Indeed the only punishment is likely to be his implied disapproval. In any case, this kind of explanation makes the greatest demands on the attention and understanding of the child, and is therefore most readily made pointless by excessive arousal in him. Needless to say, the success of any kind of talk by the adult depends upon the child's readiness to listen, and this in turn depends upon how much the child values the adult.

Field studies, especially those comparing delinquents with non-delinquents, have generally underlined the value of parental explanation, particularly of this third kind. The experimental study of its role is still in its infancy. Aronfreed (1963) has demonstrated that it tends to make children critical of themselves when they do wrong; and the same author (1968) has shown that when punishment of a relatively mild kind is accompanied by reasoning it is more effective in producing later resistance to temptation. Moreover, when punishment is explicitly related to a general rule for the child, its effects appear to be more lasting (Cheyne and Walters 1969, Parke 1969).

An unpublished experiment by Andreas (described in Cheyne and Walters 1970) has shown that explanatory talk can go a long way toward neutralizing the effect of delaying punishment. In this experiment children were punished for an offence some four hours after its occurrence. Andreas found that subsequent resistance to temptation was directly related to the extent to which the experimenter symbolically reinstated the original situation at the time of punishment.

On the basis of their own experimental work Cheyne and Walters suggest that there are two qualitatively different factors that mediate self-control in temptation situations, emotional and cognitive. They distinguish 'emotionally controlled' children, who are inhibited by high anxiety, from 'cognitively controlled' children, who are inhibited simply by recognizing that the act in question breaks some general rule they have come to understand and accept. To some extent these two kinds of self-control are incompatible, for high levels of anxiety typically prevent clear thinking; but obviously emotional control is not without cognitive elements and cognitive control is not without some minimal level of anxiety. In the normal course of development we may presume that emotional control predominates in the young child and that cognitive control progressively takes over. If this presumption is justified it follows that for older children and adolescents the most effective kind of punishment would be careful explanation of why the act is wrong; and the basic task before parent and teacher is therefore to create the kind of relationship that constrains the child to listen.

The kinds of sanction used so far in experiments hardly begin to reflect the diversity that exists in daily life. We therefore have no alternative at present but to rely upon the large number of field studies that have classified forms of punishment and established their behavioural correlates. The whole field has been excellently reviewed by Hoffman (1970) who argues that in every disciplinary act by an adult there are three basic components, each of which can predominate and can result in characteristic sorts of sanction. Each component conveys disapproval and hence each is punitive in some measure.

The first is 'power assertion'. The adult asserts an authoritative and dominant control over the child through physical punishment, fierce verbal aggression, deprivation of material privileges, angry threats, and the like. The second is 'love withdrawal'. Typically the adult shows his anger and displeasure by turning his back on the child, banishing him from his affection, refusing to speak to him, and generally isolating him. The third is 'induction'. The adult reasons with the child at length and tries to persuade him through appeals to his understanding so that he will see for himself why he was wrong. Hoffman concludes that every study reveals a negative association between predominantly power assertive discipline by parents and self-control in their children. In contrast the evidence consistently shows a positive relationship between induction and self-control. He is unable to find any consistent trend in the evidence relating love withdrawal to self-control.

Without complementary data from controlled experiments these conclusions have to be treated with caution. But there is no escaping the emphasis upon cognitive structure which the evidence brings out. If we may draw a moral from it, it is that the primary task for the adult is to create and maintain a relationship with the child such that he is liked and listened to. Then from the point of view of the child's developing conscience, all that is needed from the adult is the kind of explanation which makes clear why the act is wrong and which conveys, implicitly more than explicitly, his disapproval of it.

References

ARONFREED, J. (1963) The effects of experimental socialization paradigms upon two moral responses to transgression *Journal of Abnormal and Social Psychology* 66, 437–438

ARONFREED, J. (1968) *Conduct and Conscience* New York: Academic Press

ARONFREED, J. and REBER, A. (1965) Internal behavioural suppression and the timing of social punishment *Journal of Personality and Social Psychology* 1, 3–16

ARONSON, E. and METTEE, D. R. (1968) Dishonest behaviour as a function of differential levels of induced self-esteem *Journal of Personality and Social Psychology* 9, 121–127

BECKER, W. C. (1964) Consequences of different kinds of parental discipline *Review of Child Development Research*, vol 1

CHEYNE, J. A. and WALTERS, R. H. (1969) Timing of punishment, intensity of punishment and cognitive structure in resistance to deviation *Journal of Experimental Child Psychology* 8, 127–138

CHEYNE, J. A. and WALTERS, R. H. (1970) 'Punishment and prohibition' in K. Craik (ed) *New Directions in Psychology 4* London: Holt, Reinhart and Winston

CHURCH, R. M. (1963) The varied effects of punishment on behaviour *Psychological Review* 70, 369–402

HOFFMAN, M. L. (1970) 'Moral development' in L. Carmichael (ed) *Manual of Child Psychology* Chichester: John Wiley

PARKE, R. D. (1969) The modification of the effectiveness of punishment training by a cognitive-structuring procedure *Child Development* 40, 213–235

PARKE, R. D. and WALTERS, R. H. (1967) Some factors influencing the efficacy of punishment training for inducing response inhibition *Society for Research in Child Development Monographs*, no 109

D

SOLOMON, R. L. (1964) Punishment *American Psychologist* 19, 239–253

SOLOMON, R. L., TURNER, L. H. and LESSAC, M. S. (1968) Some effects of delay in punishment on resistance to temptation in dogs *Journal of Personality and Social Psychology* 8, 233–238

WALTERS, R. H., LEAT, M. and MESEI, H. (1963) Response inhibition and disinhibition through empathic learning *Canadian Journal of Psychology* 17, 235–243

WALTERS, R. H. and PARKE, R. D. (1964) Influence of response consequences to a social model on resistance to deviation *Journal of Experimental Child Psychology* 1, 269–280

WALTERS, R. H. and PARKE, R. D. (1968) The influence of punishment and related disciplinary techniques on the social behaviour of children *Progress in Experimental Personality Research*, vol 3

WALTERS, R. H., PARKE, R. D. and CRANE, V. A. (1965) Timing of punishment and the observation of consequences to others as determinants of response inhibition *Journal of Experimental Child Psychology* 2, 10–30

WRIGHT, D. (1971) *The Psychology of Moral Behaviour* Harmondsworth: Penguin

This paper first appeared as The punishment of children: a review of experimental studies *Journal of Moral Education*, 1, 3, June 1972, pp. 221–231, and is reproduced by kind permission of Pemberton Publishing Company.

Keith Wadd

Classroom power

Recently, a letter (Lewis 1971) in *The Times Educational Supplement* bemoaned the fact that the correspondent's Certificate of Education course had given practically no guidance in the keeping of discipline: '...surely some useful guidelines could be given to the intending teacher which might help to prevent unfortunate classroom situations'. It is doubtful if anything like a complete answer can be given to this naughty comment, but perhaps if the nature of keeping discipline is examined – how it is gained, kept and lost – it might indicate some guidelines and also shed some light on why the topic is rarely made explicit in teacher training.

Keeping discipline is bound up with the teacher's power and authority (Musgrove 1971, Fox 1971, Shipman 1969), words with unpleasant associations, which may help to account for some of the lack of serious discussion of the matter. The teacher is given authority from outside the classroom, i.e. by his employers, to influence his pupils (within certain norms). The word 'influence' is used in a very wide sense to refer to the teacher creating some change in his pupils; unless this occurs, he is merely child-minding or adolescent-minding. The extent to which the teacher's authority is accepted without challenge inside the classroom varies from a position of considerable consensus in higher and adult education where generally the pupils want to be influenced, to a situation of some conflict in junior and particularly secondary education where the pupils have more mixed feelings about being influenced. The limits of the teacher's authority in the classroom are largely a product of his personal power of which there are four main aspects: charisma (ability to attract people), dominance (ability to obtain control of a situation), intellectual power (knowledge mastery), resources power (ability to organize pupil activities). Such personal power largely determines whether the teacher's authority in the classroom is minimal or extensive. The relative importance of these types of power depends on the teaching situation, charisma being the only type which is desirable in a more or less constant amount. Thus, in higher and adult education intellectual power is of prime importance, whereas in infants teaching resources power is crucial. Junior and secondary teaching call for considerable exercise of all four types of power, the conflict situation calling for greater dominance than is usually recognized in the construction of courses in teacher training. In the discussion which follows, the analysis will mainly focus on dominance and resources power with particular reference to the junior and secondary situation. Intellectual power will be taken for granted in this paper, and charisma will be regarded as a power that few teachers have in great measure, though a great asset in any situation for those fortunate enough to possess it, since it will always add to the teacher's power. It is doubtful whether charisma can be learned, but much can be done to increase the teacher's acquisition of other types of power.

To fulfil his role of influencing his pupils, the teacher, whether he is aware of it or not, is seeking to impose a certain type of order or regime on his class, seeking to bring under his control an area of pupil behaviour as his right to punish and reward. The order has first to be established, and then maintained, though these two phases shade into each other. Establishing the order occurs during the early meetings with the pupils when the teacher gradually makes clear the type of conditions he wants, though whether he gets them is another matter; this part might be called the 'testing out' process and has been compared to bargaining (Geer 1968). The nature of the order established quickly becomes institutionalized or routinized (i.e. becomes routine), as a particular relationship between the teacher and his pupils crystallizes. It is important, because of this process of institutionalization, that the teacher establishes an order that is adequate for him effectively to influence his pupils. Maintaining order is concerned with handling threats to the amount of the teacher's power in the relationship that has been established.

It can be seen, therefore, that what is loosely called 'keeping discipline', involves the content of an order or regime, how it is established, and how it is maintained. A basic guideline regarding the content of the order will be the conditions which the teacher thinks are necessary for him effectively to influence his pupils. This means he must decide what behaviour is to be rewarded, what rewards to offer, and what restrictions to impose on pupils talking, losing attention, leaving their seats, throwing things etc. His decision will almost certainly owe something to the views of his headteacher and colleagues, and there will be limits, both upper and lower, he will be expected not to exceed – for instance, he may be expected not to exceed a certain noise level, whilst at the other end of the spectrum a too harsh regime would be criticized. There is no reason why the content of an order or regime should not be fully discussed in courses of teacher training. It is important to note that the teacher should have a clear idea of the content of the order he is seeking to establish before he comes into contact with the pupils, even though it may have to be modified in the light of circumstances. A teacher who is unsure of the order he wants, deciding to 'play it by ear', will be unsure of dealing with the threats to it that occur, or even fail to recognize them. The result will almost certainly be a pupil gain and diminished power for the teacher – 'unfortunate classroom situations' in our correspondent's words.

Both the nature of the order and the process of establishing it are intimately related to the question of legitimacy. Whatever the bounds of the order a teacher seeks to impose, his task will be far easier if the order is regarded as legitimate by his pupils; if this is so, they will respond to his rewards and regard his punishments as right. In many social contexts outside the school, considerable attention has to be given to legitimizing a regime, particularly a new regime, but this is not normally a problem in the classroom situation. However, if the teacher seeks to impose an order which makes demands on the pupils beyond what is normally acceptable in the school, a legitimacy problem occurs, and the same may be true if he is faced by a class of pupils who will concede very little. Beyond the bounds of legitimacy, a teacher must have frequent recourse to dominance – a wearisome business. Dominance is a necessary part of the teacher's repertoire, but a part to use sparingly. It is likely, however, that most pupils will accept firm control over many areas of their activity if the teacher can generate enough power to win this control. In other words, pupil norms will probably concede a wide area to the teacher, but make him fight for it.

In establishing the order he has decided on, the teacher must be fully aware that what happens in the first few encounters with the pupils is likely to establish the relationship which he will have to live with for the rest of his contact with that particular class. It is vital, therefore, that when the first challenges occur, he deals with them effectively. Let us suppose that it is essential, for his influence to be successful, that he imposes an order that requires complete pupil attention whilst he is talking (or at least complete apparent attention). The early maneuvres are crucial. With a mixture of charisma (if he has it), intellectual power, and resources power, he will proceed to unfold to his pupils the programme he has devised for them. The pupils will watch him carefully and test his order. The situation has elements of a game, but it is a power game, a struggle for power, a conflict in which the pupils are seeking albeit with mixed feelings to win a more congenial order for themselves than the teacher wants. This is not to imply that usually the pupils are organized for the challenge. Fairly soon, however, a pupil will talk to his neighbour whilst the teacher is holding forth to the class. Since this clashes with the order the teacher is seeking to establish, he must immediately be able to do something. This is where dominance is indispensable. If he fails to deal with the situation successfully, a relationship will crystallize in which he will always have to compete to be heard.

Such an incident can only be dealt with by the application of some sanction, however mild. A glare or a quiet word of rebuke may be sufficient. The situation can be compared to playing a game of bridge or whist, where normally the smallest card necessary to take the trick will be played, though in this case the virtue of playing a fairly high card might also be considered. But what happens if the card is not effective and the miscreant ignores the sanction? It is even worse if a high card has been played. This inevitably leads to a discussion of 'elementary escalation', a pupil strategy designed to see if the teacher is prepared to defend the authority he is seeking to establish and if necessary invoke higher sanctions. The implications of this very common situation might be fully explored with students – all teachers have to handle it as a regular part of their work. The writer's view is that he must use higher sanctions in this case, because he cannot afford to lose the encounter. There is a trap of course of using up all one's sanctions and being left virtually powerless – not an easy situation and one that does not only happen to the inexperienced.

One might now fruitfully discuss whether the order the teacher sought to impose in the first place was too ambitious. However, it must be remembered that he must seek to establish conditions that enable him effectively to influence his pupils. Rather than reduce the bounds of his order, he would be wise to consider the use of his resources power. If it is his aspiration that the pupils should not talk when he is talking, it will be necessary to analyse how long he is talking and what he is saying. With children and adolescents, most of whom have limited powers of concentration when called upon to listen to the spoken word enunciated by a moderate speaker, it may pay to say as little as possible and to make it effective. However, the less that is said, the more activity that has to be organized, which means that considerable attention has to be given to the organization of pupil work. If another aspect of the order the teacher seeks to impose is that the pupils shall not leave their seats without permission (leaving aside the desirability of such a rule), the teacher is likely to receive fewer challenges to his order if he meticulously prepares and organizes the work he wants the class to do, creates few opportunities for the pupils to leave their seats and continually places himself in a position to supervise. One might say therefore that high resources power reduces the number of occasions when dominance has to be used; this is true both with establishing and maintaining order.

The practical wisdom, 'It is easier to slacken off than to tighten up', introduces a further aspect of legitimacy in the process of establishing an order. The teacher whose order controls many areas of pupil behaviour is in a position to concede minor areas without serious loss; he is in a stronger position of course if the concession is made by his power, and not obtained by a successful exercise of his pupils' power. In fact towards the end of a course greater permissiveness is often used as a reward. The other side of the coin, and it is very important, is that what has not been established at the outset as being the teacher's legitimate order, cannot subsequently be imposed without a severe power struggle that the teacher is likely to lose. The pupils will challenge the new area since an attempt is being made to outlaw behaviour that was previously regarded as legitimate for them. Hence the difficulties of the inexperienced teacher who, like a lamb to the slaughter, has gone into the classroom thinking that the pupils will like him, find the work he has for them very stimulating, his voice and ideas very attractive etc. Well as he has prepared his work, the volume of noise rises in the class; interesting as his activities are the pupils throw things when he is not looking. In despair he announces with regret, 'We will stop talking!' and in greater despair finds he is completely unable to enforce his demands. His error was that he had failed to establish an order suitable for the effective use of his resources; later, when he attempted to impose such an order, it was not regarded as legitimate. It can further be suggested from this example that high resources power without dominance is likely to leave the teacher ineffective.

The process of maintaining order is in many ways less of a problem than that of establishing it. This is because the teacher is at this stage operating in a context in which the relationship between himself and the class has crystallized. It is now clear how far the teacher's order extends. Dominance is still needed of course as the pupils will still sometimes trespass on his domain. But they will regard his punishments and rewards as legitimate provided that they broadly conform with the sort of relationship that has been established. The most important aspect of maintaining order, however, involves the use of resources power. As we have seen, the higher the resources power, the fewer the occasions for the use of dominance; the weaker the resources power the more occasions the class get restless and in various ways threaten the order that has been established. One can bring in at this stage a Parsonian model (Parsons 1959) which sees the pupils making demands and the teacher receiving further support if he satisfies these demands; the demands here are for the teacher's resources power and intellectual power, and the pupils are likely to withdraw support if the demands are not broadly met.

A model of 'keeping discipline' has now been sketched out; the question of why practically no guidance in keeping discipline has been given to the intending teacher can next be examined. Actually, it is almost certainly incorrect to talk of 'practically no guidance', but it would not be outrageous to suggest that the guidance that is given is probably insufficiently explicit in some areas and inadequate in others.

One reason for this state of affairs is that nonauthoritarian norms in institutions of teacher education have hindered the full recognition of the obvious fact that the teacher, whether he likes it or not, is in a position of authority and needs to be fully powered for such a position. Another reason is that courses of teacher training have tended to operate from the starting point of passing on knowledge (Geer 1968), or the developing child, and have largely overlooked the matter of the pupil rejecting much of the knowledge, or not wanting to develop in a way that is entirely consistent with the teacher's ideas. It is not surprising that such courses have turned out teachers who are unarmed for the numerous conflict situations that arise in their work. Another failing is an overemphasis on rapport; there is a vast difference between those who have the gift of charismatic leadership, and those who can manage little more than ineffective congeniality. Overemphasis on resources power is another inadequate approach, though a less serious one; a teacher whose resources are so good that they eliminate the use of dominance is some sort of superman who is certainly not to be found amongst teachers at the beginning of their careers if indeed he is to be found anywhere at all. The general weakness of all these approaches to keeping discipline is that they are based upon an inadequate analysis of the problem and hence prescribe (where they are explicit on the matter at all) an exaggerated emphasis on just one of the factors involved. Not only is there a discrepancy between theory and practice, the theory itself is faulty. The accumulated wisdom of the school staffroom probably has far more to offer.

Before this paper is concluded, a discussion is required of some consensus approaches to keeping discipline. Consensus is nearly always a desirable thing to strive for in teaching, since in creating more common ground, it reduces the conflict, makes the pupils more responsive to the teachers' intellectual and resources power, and reduces the occasions for the use of dominance. Those teachers fortunate enough to have charisma will of course find consensus easy to obtain. In an age when existing authority is challenged and the need for any authority is disputed, consensus approaches are popular, particularly with students who feel uncomfortable in any authority position. There is one trap in the consensus approach which the inexperienced should be warned against. This is the attempt to gain consensus by refusing to use dominance. The result of this will be the crystallization of convivial chaos from which very little effective teaching will emerge; possibly a genuinely charismatic teacher might rescue the situation, but it is mere vanity for most people to expect this. Consensus alone will not teach; effective teaching springs from consensus on the teacher's authority – which is a very different thing. Most approaches to obtaining more consensus, however, do not put this authority at risk. An obvious method is by modifying the syllabus and curriculum in order to make the teaching more apparently relevant; curriculum reform obviously comes into this category. The less relevant a subject, the more power of all sorts that needs to be generated for teaching it; for example, Musgrove (1971) points out, 'Only a strong man should venture to teach scripture anywhere.' There are also various 'architectural' methods of trying to achieve more consensus, having in common the aim of placing teacher and pupils as little as possible in a position of direct confrontation. Informal grouping of desks is one way, and another approach is building schools to an open plan which avoids the formal classroom situation as much as possible. Another method of this type is extending the range of pupil activities beyond the confines of classroom and school (deschooling is in this category), in order to limit the opportunities for conflict and to introduce activities that might seem more relevant. Another well-known method of increasing consensus is the 'democratic' approach which is designed to give the pupils more apparent control over their work. It must be stressed, however, that most of these approaches are beyond the reach of most teachers most of the time; most teachers struggle on in the traditional classroom with an imaginative (one hopes) use of the limited resources available to them, laced with a little dominance where necessary. It is not surprising perhaps that the demands of the conflict situation are such that a further strategy for obtaining consensus has sometimes been adopted, the sell-out. Here, the teacher by making big concessions, restricts the area of authority he wishes to establish over the pupils, but in consequence his influence is much impaired. This situation has been well described by Hargreaves (1967). It is not so much a trap that the innocent blindly falls into, as a condition that afflicts the weary and cynical.

To avoid misunderstanding of this article, some final points must be made. Firstly, though it is written from a keeping discipline perspective, it is certainly not being suggested that discipline is of supreme importance in the classroom situation; it is the quality of the teacher's influence that is most important. Secondly, the discussion is not intended to be an apologia for authoritarianism. This claim rests upon a distinction being made between authoritarianism and wielding authority. The teacher's role in any society is inextricably bound up with power and authority; however, authoritarianism might be considered as occurring if the teacher uses dominance to mask a deficiency of intellectual and resources power, or if he attempts to coerce pupils into a regime which is harsher than might normally be regarded as legitimate, or if he controls pupil behaviour that is in no way a threat to his teaching effectiveness. The distinction is broadly one between use and abuse of authority. Finally, the use of 'progressive' methods is in no way invalidated by the theme of this article. But it would be hypocritical to pretend that they are not a form of power; it would be unwise not to consider the type of order they require if they are to flourish.

In conclusion, the exercise of power and authority is an inescapable part of the teacher's role, whatever the type of teaching he is involved in. In particular, the working lives of most teachers are concerned with trying to generate enough power of various sorts to obtain the authority to teach effectively in a conflict situation. One suspects that there has been a reluctance explicitly to recognize this fact in the construction of courses of teacher training, and related to this a failure to explore the nature of power and authority in the classroom situation. It is hoped the model developed in this article will assist a better understanding of the matter. At present, the help that is given to the intending teacher tends to assume he is a sort of resources superman or charismatic magician who can establish his order without challenge, and in addition assumes a state of consensus that rarely exists in most teaching. In consequence, the intending teacher has been encouraged to fly before he can walk, and it is little wonder that he has often got hurt in the process. Such an experience can easily lead to much of the process of teacher training being regarded as largely irrelevant.

References

Fox, A. (1971) *A Sociology of Work in Industry* New York: Collier-Macmillan

Geer, B. (1968) 'Teaching' in *International Encyclopedia of the Social Sciences* volume 15 New York: Collier-Macmillan

Hargreaves, D. H. (1967) *Social Relations in a Secondary School* London: Routledge and Kegan Paul

Lewis, R. P. (1971) Letter in *The Times Educational Supplement* 17th December

Musgrove, F. (1971) *Patterns of Power and Authority in English Education* London: Methuen

Parsons, T. (1959) 'General theory in sociology' in R. K. Merton *et al* (eds) *Sociology Today* New York: Basic Books

Shipman, M. D. (1969) *The Sociology of the School* London: Longman

This paper first appeared in *Education for Teaching*, Autumn 1972, pp. 42–50 and is reproduced by kind permission of The Association of Teachers in Colleges and Departments of Education.

Barry Turner

Pride and prejudice

As headteachers of nervous disposition never tire of reminding us, education is a reflection of society. In the midst of crisis their shrill voices can be heard: 'We at least are not to blame.' And they have a case, a small one it is true, but one that is nonetheless worth stating. When a school has problems in asserting its institutional authority, when pupils consistently transgress the most basic rules of behaviour and when the actual business of learning is treated like a sideshow joke, then it is a reasonable guess that the mood of disaffection embraces the wider community. So also on a national level, if a significant proportion of the school and college generation react to traditional moral and social values with an equally traditional gesture of contempt (and for the moment it is irrelevant whether you happen to think this is a good or a bad thing), it is nonsense to assume, as so many observers seem to suggest, that the sole responsibility belongs to the educators.

Consider what has happened over the last decade. Young people have questioned, criticized and in some cases demolished values and standards practised, or at any rate tolerated, by every previous generation of the century. Perhaps because we are part of the change it is not easy to assess the impact of this revolution except in the most obvious terms – the permissive society, pupil power, the generation gap, and so on. But the emotive force that gives some sort of reality and life to these clichés is the attitude of the under 30s and, more particularly, the under 20s to conventional authority. In a word – they do not like it and what they do not like they have a tendency to hit out at, to ignore, or possibly most hurtful of all, to dismiss in a gust of rude laughter.

But who inspires this show of antiauthoritarian solidarity? The teacher? Well, yes, he is undoubtedly partly responsible if only by virtue of performing his proper function of raising the standards of literacy to a level where authority is no longer accepted on trust. A few years ago most young people – and adults too for that matter – were prepared to do as they were told because they did not have the understanding or knowledge to think of an alternative. But latterly questions have been asked and reasons demanded and when the replies have not been forthcoming with the alacrity that might be expected from social leaders who are apparently confident of their power to determine right and wrong, the new generation have looked for and sometimes found their own answers. This has already happened in the area of sex relationships, where traditional attitudes are so beset with prejudice and hypocrisy that even the most lucid defenders of the old values lose themselves in the intricacy of their own verbal gyrations.

Along with the intellectual independence nurtured by the educators – and not least by those who now are heard most frequently calling for a return to earlier, decent standards of conformity and discipline – must go the sense of economic freedom created by the technologists and their support force of administrators and salesmen. In the modern industrial society most young people can earn or expect to earn a living that is well above the subsistence level. Their work (in the factory as in school) may be frequently uninspiring but it is compensated by an escape into youth culture that is itself the product of economic prosperity and the cause of misunderstanding and conflict between the generations. The adoption of new fashions in language, dress, music or whatever can be, and often is, interpreted as a deliberate assault upon the settled standards of the ruling elders and thus as a source of disruption and indiscipline.

Then there are the communicators – the news, views and ideas people who enjoy unprecedented opportunities for self-expression. Much of their energy is spent in pulling away the veils – often several layers thick – from the power structure of society. What is revealed is frequently unappealing especially to a generation that does not feel the compulsion to earn approval by politely ignoring the defects of its masters. Thus the politician of a few years ago who had only to show his face to earn a rousing chorus of For He's a Jolly Good Fellow may now be portrayed as a self-seeking little squit whose sole contribution to the social order is to show that lack of principles and conviction need not disqualify a candidate for a remunerative profession. There are those who would argue that the last few years have offered far better than average chances for belabouring authority, that the leaders in all the old established departments of society – politics, the Church, law and education – are generally inferior to their predecessors. But a likelier explanation is that their defects are more readily detectable, if only because television – the most popular and powerful debunking medium of them all – gives them greater opportunities for making fools of themselves.

The disillusionment with politics is not, of course, the prerogative of youth. Indeed it is probable that the mood of cynicism which now identifies the school and college generation, originated with the parents who in company with the educators, technologists and communicators must share the responsibility for launching the antiauthoritarian movement among the young.

After all, the political assertion that meets with the broadest consent is that our society lacks any sense of purpose. The argument was expressed in its most grandiose terms by Dean Acheson, who said that Britain had lost an empire and had not yet found a role (a sentiment that set off so much nervous anger it just had to be true). But if adult society no longer has the ability to excite or to be excited it is really not surprising that young people should fail to respond to the Dunkirk rallying call or thrill to reports of mean political squabbles.

But if it is possible to deduce the origins of dissatisfaction among young people, what can be said of the way it manifests itself, particularly in the education system? The first thing to be said is that of all the antiauthoritarian reactions, violence is the least popular and certainly the least effective, even though it achieves maximum publicity. Everyone has had a vicarious acquaintance with the Mods and Rockers, Hells Angels, or the Angry Brigade because the thuggish activities of such groups appeal to the dramatic instincts of the communicators and their audiences. But it is a long jump from enjoying a punch up on television or thrilling to the report of an imaginative newspaperman, to actually participating in destructive adventures. For one thing it is common understanding that violence against established authority will necessarily provoke a stronger counter reaction which makes eventual defeat almost inevitable.

This elementary fact determines the behaviour of a child in school or a student at college every bit as much as it influences the tactics of extremist political groups. But, more significantly, violence simply does not have the emotional or the intellectual appeal for this generation that many of the elders seem to imagine. Yet, so obsessed are they with the fear of an imminent breakdown of the social order in an orgy of delinquency that they refuse even to believe the findings of their own research.

Thus, the NAS Report *Violence in Schools* (Lowenstein 1972), with its superfluity of negative evidence, is reminiscent of the famous essay *Snakes in Ireland* which consisted of the single line, 'There are no snakes in Ireland.' Of 4,800 secondary schools which were asked to report on violent behaviour (this covered every conceivable manifestation of aggression from gang fighting to 'rudeness to headmaster') less than 1,100 bothered even to return the questionnaires. Of these about 600 reported violence of some kind, but only sixty-six admitted to serious problems while at the other end of the scale 401 schools said they experienced violence infrequently or very infrequently.

More widespread than any form of violence is the technique which is roughly equivalent to what the army used to call dumb insolence. Many youngsters are highly skilled in the exercise of applied apathy, refusing to show more than minimum interest in any scholastic activity while reserving their energy for pursuits beyond the school walls. These are not troublesome characters – at least they usually keep quiet in class – but teachers are sometimes hurt and surprised to find, say, that a boy who is not at all inclined to join in organized sports on behalf of his school will derive immense pleasure from kicking a ball about on a demolition site with his mates.

The braver souls are more openly defiant, refusing to obey rules which seem to them to be unjustified or just plain silly and asserting their own choices of behaviour even when these are known to conflict with the expectations of the institution and the community. These disputes can accelerate into open warfare, as many college and university administrators will unhappily testify, but it is difficult not to conclude that excesses could be avoided if only educators would bother less about their own sense of self-importance. One of the common features of these confrontations is the thrusting, determined jaw of a teacher or administrator who likes to think of himself as a lone defender of the faith against the asaults of the barbaric hordes and who believes, apparently sincerely, that to give way a single inch will be interpreted as a sign of fatal weakness heralding total defeat for decency and justice.

And it is not only educators who possess this failing. Among the more ludicrous misunderstandings between the generations is the running dispute (now thankfully almost played out) on the question of what is or is not a proper form of dress for young people. Just about everyone has had something to say on this topic, but some of the harshest critics of the more extravagant fashions have been those who themselves are inclined to adopt unusual styles of costume. Eminent among the recent defenders of convential attire have been a judge, who presumably takes some pride in displaying himself in a powdered wig, a headteacher who signifies his academic distinction by appearing on television in a full-length gown, and a bishop of the Church of England who, resplendent in a black dress and high boots, looks for all the world like a practising advocate of unisex for the elderly.

Young people are by no means slow to catch on to such paradoxes, but it is perhaps a welcoming sign of generosity that they usually react with good humour – a characteristic that some of their critics might do well to emulate. Instead they seem to get wilder and angrier in their accusations, which only serves to improve their entertainment value. Thus, to return for a moment to the ever interesting topic, the prophets of antisex, who appear to believe that their message has a special significance for the young, are a source of huge enjoyment for the masses. Longford, Muggeridge and Whitehouse, those purveyors of Christian purity in an age when more and more people are asking what Christian purity has ever done for them, promise to become the most popular comedy team on television. The tragedy and the irony of the situation is that they do not give any impression of realizing their predicament.

Most or all of these reflections may have already occurred to the involved teacher, who might reasonably ask how in sheer practical terms they can be of help in the exercise of classroom management. Certainly, they do not lead to a set of fool-proof rules for good teaching (though other contributors to this book may satisfy that need); but if it is accepted that young people are assuming an independence of spirit they will not easily surrender and that in an open society which has aspirations to becoming a participating democracy this could actually be a positive and hopeful development, then at least we can start talking sensibly about what not to do. And the first and most important thing not to do is to act as if every child is a potential delinquent in need of corrective treatment. It is staggering how many teachers still believe that their job is three quarters done if they can create an environment of fear.

This is an older master talking a short time ago to an interviewer from *The Teacher*: 'If the whole school decides to get up and walk out there's nothing any of the teachers can do. Mind you, I know what I'd do. I'd pick on the ten roughest boys in the school and I'd give them hell. In a school, as in society, you must have order. Permissiveness? Personally, I think that's just a euphemism for immorality. A child must never be allowed to get away with outright disobedience. Never.'

And now a more recent recruit to the profession: 'Some of them can be really obscene and try to touch you. You cannot just ignore it. I've found the best policy is to behave as you would if you were outside school. I've given some of them a good hard slap, and it seems to work. They know that "She'll hit you if you go too far".'

Good heavens girls, what did they teach you at college? That if any child touches you strike out as if you have been attacked by a homicidal maniac?

But don't let us be too hard. Teachers who live on their nerves because they are frightened of losing the power of one-upmanship can be found in any school in the country. Perhaps in the long run the answer is to provide teachers with a greater knowledge of psychology and sociology – even to train teachers and social workers in the same colleges – so that schools can acquire a better idea of how they influence their pupils, how group dynamics work, how particular groups of children are motivated and what they and their culture have to offer, and how conflicts can be resolved.

The expansion of in-service training may provide opportunities in this direction. Then we might be able to get away from the idea that youngsters are simply plasticine creatures to be moulded into sober and obedient citizens. Meanwhile, let us relax a little, remember that most kids have something worthwhile to offer, and that just occasionally it may be worthwhile listening to their ideas instead of talking at them.

References
LOWENSTEIN, L. F. (1972) *Violence in Schools* Hemel Hempstead: NAS

Ron Cocking

School and society

Many people today, and I am one of them, believe that problems of maintaining school order are becoming more difficult. There should be no surprise at this situation. Society itself is changing and authority is under attack. Society has changed before. Once primitive people fought for food, women, homes or fuel. As civilization grew the need for laws to regulate the action of individuals and groups in a community was recognized. Laws were made and were given an aura of holiness because they were necessary to enable society to survive. But inevitably there were those who felt they were treated unjustly. They challenged the laws, often by force.

Now whether or not such action is justified, there is the problem that when some sections of society see laws undermined they perceive profit for themselves in the challenge itself and act without regard to consequence. When violence is seen to bring advantage violence increases. This is what is happening today. Young people see the examples of violence and the successful challenge to authority and they tend to emulate it without even the justification of misguided idealism. The communications media, in attempting to present the news objectively, give violence and disruption a tacit acceptance and do not condemn it. Youngsters seeing it uncondemned come to regard it as acceptable.

Children today are treated with a tolerance which allows for the rejection of authority. Paradoxically parents are often critical of lax school discipline whilst tolerating behaviour at home which would not have been widely accepted twenty years ago. Even more difficult to understand, they question and oppose steps which might make school discipline more effective.

Children brought up in a tolerant atmosphere at home are often shocked by atempts to make them behave reasonably in school. They find themselves having to adopt two quite different behaviour patterns. This can have a traumatic effect upon some children which is in itself an incitement to indiscipline.

The problem about any examination of discipline in the schools is that it involves two basic propositions which in a sense are contradictory. The first is that society accepts that education to be effective must be conducted in a reasonably ordered situation. Society as a whole appears to accept that the majority of children want to learn and that to enable them to do so discipline must be maintained in the learning institutions. There are those, extreme liberals and the supporters of revolution for its own sake, who may not share that view but they do not appear to have affected the opinion of the majority. The second proposition is that schools cannot in this age operate in isolation; whatever happens and whatever is tolerated in the world has an effect in our schools. The attitudes of adults with whom pupils come into contact, either by direct experience or through communications media, condition the attitude of the pupils to all influences on their lives.

Until recently the few children who disrupted schools with extreme behavioural problems came from environments which thrived on violence and misbehaviour. But the growth of mass communications media, especially the visual ones, and the decline of censorship has introduced a much wider group to extremes of behaviour. Thus, a society which expects and believes that its children must be educated in a reasonably ordered situation tolerates the daily visual exposition of activities which can undermine and destroy that reasonable order.

This may be a very stark way of defining a very complex problem, but the complexities are very often used to confuse the position and truth can sometimes be concealed by too great heed being given to marginal considerations. The problem for education emerging from the contradiction is simply this: when schools attempt to maintain the reasonable order which society wants, the support of our society is conditional. And in the long run that situation is intolerable.

In a school where there is mutual respect between teachers and pupils, almost any normal measure of disciplinary enforcement is accepted. In another where parental relationships are poor, and the school receives scant respect, any measure of enforcement is likely to be challenged. Parental involvement and understanding is vital to the school whether the disciplinary measures used in the school are physical or nonphysical. The extent of parental involvement is important both in the avoidance of extreme indiscipline and to its solution when it occurs.

At this point it should be made clear that in my view the question of the type of enforcement used is irrelevant. I do not intend to enter into the corporal punishment controversy except to say that the danger of abolishing a particular form of punishment by legislation fails to recognize that teachers or anyone else for that matter, are conditioned by their experiences. Legislation to hurry along a situation that is not developing as quickly as some people would like is dangerous when it is applied to human relationships. You cannot suddenly by law change a teacher who, through experience and service in particular schools, has accepted the necessity to use corporal punishment. Neither can you change by law children who have been conditioned to accept caning as a proper result of misbehaviour. The process of change is slow and the action in respect of it must be gradual.

The point of course is emphasized when one considers further the whole relationship of teacher, child and parent. A child who comes from a home in which corporal punishment is a norm for misbehaviour is uneasy in a school where the cane is not used. A child who comes from a home where corporal punishment is unheard of (and there are fewer of these than some people think) and becomes a pupil in a school where such punishment is used finds difficulty in adjustment. Opinion might be that the second child would settle more easily than the first, but that of course is the result of pressures to conform supported by a forceful punishment policy.

The consideration of these points enters into the question of discipline in schools only when one considers methods rather than effects, except in one respect; if one accepts that violence breeds violence in a society where authority is constantly questioned, then it might be acceptable that the abandonment of violence by authority may diminish the aggression of those who challenge authority. But there certainly appears to be some basis for the opposite conclusion, that the use of violence by authority only increases the violent reaction of those challenging authority until authority amasses enough power to overwhelm its challengers. It is of course equally true to say that the removal of authority violence in a society which, even if reluctantly, accepts the violence of power, leaves the reasonable population with no defences and no foundation.

But to return to my two basic propositions. At the moment we have the curious situation where society produces its own pressures which operate against the maintenance of that reasonable order in schools which society regards as necessary for education. The results of this contradiction can be seen in what is clearly an increasing amount of violence and disruptive behaviour in schools.

During 1971/2 in one large education authority area 126 children were suspended out of a total of 180,000 children. This is a very small minority of the school population and no one would wish to pretend otherwise. These 126 were obviously suspended because they were causing difficulty or disruption which required drastic action but not all were violent. But it is interesting to note some of the descriptions of these cases recorded in reports to governing bodies: Boy 11 Suspended for 'violent and provocative behaviour'; Girl 10 'Suspended for disruptive behaviour'; Boy 14 'Unruly behaviour culminating in a vicious attack on fellow pupil'; Boy 5 'Disturbed and frightening behaviour'; Boy 15 'Disruptive behaviour culminating in vicious attack on fellow pupil'; Boy 11 'Violent behaviour toward fellow pupils'; Boy 11 'Bullying and assaulting younger children and foul and abusive language'; Boy 12 'Violent attack on another pupil'.

It would be instructive to obtain comparative figures over the last twenty years but it is not easy to do. However education committee members who are questioned on this will admit that figures were much lower a decade ago and that the nature of the cases was very different. Boys, for instance, often came to blows but the use of vicious weapons and the boot on a fallen opponent were regarded as cowardly and unacceptable. Today children will kick and strike out with any object. Some carry dangerous weapons and are willing to use them. Many a teacher has been threatened with a knife by a child. More important, liberal attitudes among adults have probably given encouragement to these youngsters who have violent or disruptive inclinations.

A teacher in a Bristol comprehensive school was attacked in the chemistry room by two boys aged thirteen and fourteen. He did not retaliate and was punched in the face and struck by the two boys. They had been suspended from their class and felt they had a grievance. The teacher was almost killed. His skull was fractured and he had an emergency operation to remove a blood clot near the brain. He emerged with a speech disability. The boys admitted causing grievous bodily harm and were sent to a detention centre for three months with one year's 'after care'. The chairman of the school governors said, 'If the teacher does not recover his speech we shall have to declare a vacancy.' When challenged about the leniency of the sentence, the chairman of the court panel commented, 'One has to remember *these boys have to live in society* when they come out.' One can only comment that perhaps the sentence should have been long enough for some ascertainment to be made of their fitness to live in society.

In a recent case a headteacher who suspended a boy for continual misdemeanour was not only let down badly by his governors but found that the boy received such publicity from the incident that he almost began a film career on the strength of it. Only the good sense of the actors' union prevented this encouragement to the rebellious. Another boy whose intemperate and unjustified criticism of his school reflects an unfortunate attitude which could affect him adversely in later life was made the star turn one evening on the David Frost programme.

It would be wrong to give the impression that all local education authorities fail to support their schools on this issue. Some do so with great firmness. In London, the ILEA have recently agreed to set up centres for temporary training for children whose disruptive attitude has led to them being excluded from the schools at which they are registered. At these centres they will be members of smaller groups than is normal, with teachers specially selected for their ability to help such difficult pupils. This is a constructive attempt to deal with a problem which some people would rather pretend does not exist.

Some LEAs have a fine record of giving consistent backing to the professionals. The large urban authority cited earlier as having 126 children suspended in a year is one in which the teachers are supported by the LEA. These authorities are to be commended.

But so often children who run amok in London schools somehow ensure that television cameras are well placed to record their ravings and racing, and to give them an impression that such actions are acceptable, and indeed worthy. Is it any wonder that teachers are concerned as to the way one can reasonably enforce order in schools?

They look to the United States and find no comfort there; they see only the difficulty into which undue tolerance can lead. There the argument began (as it has begun here) with disputes over uniform. The discussion ran like this: It is not right to impose teachers' ideas of hair length on the children. It is not right to impose ideas on dress (uniform) on the children. It is not right to impose ideas on personal behaviour on the children. It is not right to impose *anything* on children and this includes reasonable behaviour, moral standards, personal standards, performance norms, examinations, timetables, rules in school or out, in fact anything which the child does not originate becomes an imposition.

Give way on point one and it is difficult to hold point two and so on. People who have experienced education in the States in 1972 report that the final stage has been reached in many American schools. And we are on the same track.

Can anything be done to change this situation in society at a stage when the questioning of a child's right to make all decisions in a vacuum is allowed? Is a teacher or a parent permitted to put a view based on a longer experience of life? Are teachers supported when they put their increasing difficulty before society? Would the communications media be willing to present the problem with a fair projection of those who try to maintain decent standards instead of always appearing to despise those who wish to maintain a stable society? If the answer to these questions is generally yes, then I believe there is a chance to avoid a breakdown in our educational system and our own society. According to Toynbee, nineteen out of twenty-one civilizations have collapsed from within. They were not overthrown by conquerors; they simply rotted. Ours could go the same way and there are signs that we could be at this stage saying, 'It could not happen here' – with some trepidation in our voices because we all realize it might. It is therefore vital to examine ways in which the responsible and concerned sections of society can most easily avert disaster. Schools are concerned about children, so are most parents, the juvenile courts, social workers, child care officers, and responsible older pupils. All these agencies can play some part in ensuring that reasonable order is maintained in our schools.

The school must first accept that it cannot operate on its own in dealing with rebellious pupils, and that its best allies should be the parents. This is not to suggest that it is only when trouble arises that one contacts parents. Parental assistance is most valuable when it has been built up on a basis of mutual respect. The school which seeks every possible opportunity to involve parents will find when the crises come that parents will help. They will come in as equal partners not as the defenders of their wayward children. If there is a history of consideration of their point of view by the school then they know that the teacher is saying to them, 'Our Johnny has a problem, what can *we* do about it?' not '*Your* boy's in trouble, what do *you* intend to do about it?' The second question is often stupid because there is little they can directly do except to take the boy to a different school.

If the parents are involved, are consulted early and are asked to help, then the divisions which children can exploit between home and school are less likely to be created. If the parents are totally indifferent and have not been found cooperative in spite of many attempts by the school, the approach should not be different but it may be more difficult. On the other hand, the sympathetic approach may well be the basis of a new understanding between parent and teacher. It must be recognized however, that unless this rapid parental involvement becomes an accepted norm then the banishment of certain disciplinary procedures still available to teachers becomes less, not more, possible.

In the end the responsibility for the child's behaviour must be borne by the parent. To have a child who is recognized as badly behaved in school by both parents and teachers must be regarded as a matter of serious social concern. In countries which have abandoned corporal punishment this social concern has emerged as a vital matter in maintaining some sort of order in school. On the continent behaviour is seen as the concern of the parent; education that of the teacher. There might be some move toward that understanding in this country with advantage to school.

It is true that some pupils resist parental pressure but I wonder whether the children who do this are not protesting against a change in parental concern when they have already been allowed to go too far. Families which express their concern for a child by real care for its well being, by reasoning with the child, by instilling moral and behavioural standards in a way that the child accepts, by being really concerned if a child lets them down in small ways initially, have a better chance of influencing a child than the family which has regard only for material provision even on the most lavish scale and which neglects the real care which a child needs. It could be that the evidence of parental concern raised by teachers could have the effect of influencing pupils because it could indicate parental involvement which has not been obvious before. Certainly however, parental involvement is vital. From then on if the difficult behavioural pattern continues, at least home and school could work together. Even decisions about acceptable punishments should be mutual; supported and even administered by both parties.

But there comes the point though, whether or not parents cooperate, where the pupil is causing such disruption that education of other children is being affected. Here the professional decision-making right of the headteacher has to be accepted, but the parents must still be involved. To get the parents up to school and to inform them that their child has gone so far that suspension is necessary is the only method. To send a boy home with a message or to inform parents by post or by an intermediary is provocative in the extreme.

On the spot suspension is rarely necessary, but when it is unavoidable the child should be taken home by the head and the matter discussed with the parents. The parents have the right to know what suspension means and what follows in each case. They must know what steps they may take to make the child acceptable in school again, whether it happens to be the school from which he has been suspended or another one. They also have a right to know what the headteacher is suggesting to the LEA as further action. Is the child being referred to child guidance personnel, social workers, recommended for a move to another school or classed as ineducable in normal school?

At this point the LEA have to recognize that they have a responsibility to the teacher as well as to the child. Some LEAs take the view that they can pass responsibility to a teacher and then that is the end of it. This is nonsense. Without question, the LEA is responsible for supporting the teacher when he exercises that responsibility. To suggest for instance that a headteacher unreasonably suspends a child would, in my view, be nonsensical. A decision to suspend any child is taken carefully, on professional grounds, studying behavioural patterns over a long period. For an LEA to so question the professional judgment of a headteacher in putting out of school, temporarily, a very badly behaved child is a questioning of their own judgment in appointing heads. LEAs must back heads initially and then proceed to make available all the support services necessary to help the child.

What really now requires examination is the nature and effectiveness of the support services. It could be that a proper examination of what can be done for the disruptive and/or violent pupil is necessary. Certainly the increase in the number of violent children may force a complete examination of how we deal with them when they so utterly reject school order as to have to be rejected by school. There must be some special provision made for them. No one has really examined what can be provided for the pupil of average intelligence who is not disturbed or physically handicapped but who categorically rejects normal behavioural patterns. It is not enough to find another headteacher to take on the problem which will be a burden to his staff until the pupil's rejection affects that school too. Nor is it necessarily appropriate for a disruptive child to be sent to a school for maladjusted children because this type of difficulty may not be easily dealt with in such a school.

Suggestions have been made of facing these pupils with situations in which discipline is imposed by forces beyond human control. Outward bound courses, in which the pupil who does not accept those rules which enable one to face the elements would find discomfort or danger, have been suggested and there may be some good sense in this approach.

The answer which is most harmful of course is the continual acceptance of the behavioural problem as the least of many evils. We could be creating our own problems by attempting to compromise with our pupils on standards. In consultations with people who have seen the trend in the States it quickly becomes apparent how situations can deteriorate. Pupils in this country are now saying 'It is an affront to dignity to attempt to impose hair length or type of clothing on teenagers.' Many people now see this as reasonable but it does become more difficult to impose restrictions on language, sexual activity, laziness, or any mode of behaviour. This argument has, I have already indicated, been lost in many American schools where staff find themselves unable to assert any influence for what they regard as reason, because students can reject their idea of reason as imposition. What America did yesterday, we do today; even to the extent of committing the same mistakes. If we argue otherwise, experience is against us.

No one knows completely the answers to the problem of maintaining good order in schools. It may come through a return to some very firm authority; it may come through a new form of school democracy. It *will* come because society will demand good order because of the massive national investment in our schools. What is absolutely certain is that schools cannot operate on their own. This is a social problem which cannot be disregarded by society and left to the schools. Neither must the schools assume that the teaching profession alone can deal with it. In some circumstances, the problem goes outside the school when the school tries to prevent it doing so and is then wrongly slanted or distorted because of attempts to repress it.

Society must face up to the problem society is creating. Tolerance, overindulgence, neglect of standards, abandonment of guidance, unwillingness to accept and reason are social attitudes which are affecting the schools. At the same time social neglect in poor housing, unemployment, deprivation, family needs for income from both mother and father, the lack of provision for community occupation are also likely to stimulate and foster the development of bad attitudes. The schools cannot operate in a vacuum neither can they be expected to cure all society's ills even when full cooperation is provided. It is no earthly use telling a child from a home where both parents go out to work, from a house which is shared with ageing parents and uncle's family too, who is expected to play or find experience of life in a downtown area, and who knows of the gross unfairness of the provision in different schools, that he lives in the freest country in the world and then expect him to utilize that freedom in the same way as the respectable middle class child. It is also useless to preach this freedom to middle class children and then to expect any one of them who is socially aware not to be questioning and to want to utilize the freedom for some idealistic aim. It is useless to expect all children to be totally unaffected by unsophisticated revolutionary thinking which leads to actions unacceptable to the reasonable part of society, and the most susceptible are those who perceive the contradictions in our own society.

This kind of thinking may lead one to very different conclusions about what may be done to alleviate the violence occurring in schools at this time, but the thinking really does involve long-term plans for social change. The fact is however that schools have their problems now. They are increasing now. They must be dealt with and society must supply the support to the schools and for the schools now.

This is not hysteria. This is a demand which involves the protection of the well-being of the majority of children who want to get the best out of the very effective educational provision we make now. If investment in our children's education is investment in our society's future then society had better safeguard its investment by supporting those to whom it has entrusted the realization of its children's talents.

R. F. Mackenzie

Teachers of the world unite

Much discussion centres on the plight of the teacher facing a hostile class, subject to the professional taunt of not being able to quell the class, humiliated by the continuing noise, trying hard to be reasonable and fair, to present an interesting lesson, to help the pupils, and being driven through a length of distressing days and sleepless nights into despair. The Black Bookmakers say that all the trouble comes from a militant minority of pupils. If we had the guts to 'discipline' these, our troubles in the classroom would be over.

The revolt in the classroom is following the pattern of most revolts. I am sure that the Romans, chaining up their field slaves in their kennels for the night, when the name of Spartacus was just a fearful rumour, preached the same sharp lesson for dealing with incipient mutiny among the slaves. A good flogging would decrease the influence of the militants and bring the docile to heel. More force was the beginning and the end of their ingenuity. Throughout history that seemed to be all right, as long as it worked. The slaves built the pyramids, ploughed the fields, rowed the galleys, picked the cotton.

It is not all right today. It will not work. But it is perhaps the most significant characteristic of our decaying civilization that so many of its prefects still believe that they can win by the use of force.

Why is it that so many educationists, kind, intelligent, cultured and sensitive people, believe in the use of force in the classroom? One reason is that they have been misled by the use of the word *discipline*.

I sometimes warn my pupils that there are some words which have no corresponding reality behind them. Years ago, attending education conferences, whenever a speaker used the word discipline, I would ask him to define the word. I collected the definitions, and they were so varied that I reached the conclusion that discipline is a fabricated word with no attendant reality. Somebody said that God gave man language so that he could conceal his thoughts. When I hear the word discipline I suspect that something devious may be going on under this smokescreen.

When you penetrate the smoke surrounding the word discipline, you usually discover corporal punishment; the words are nearly interchangeable. The educationists who say there should be more discipline generally mean that there should be more corporal punishment. But discipline has a more respectable, cultured air about it; it suggests the serenity of the moral philosophy lecture hall, not the anger of the classroom, the youngster with arm outstretched, the teacher bringing the leather down sharply on the open hand. The physical pain of corporal punishment should not be obtrusive; so it is obscured behind the abstract term, discipline.

A better-educated élite would have been forewarned against this word. It comes straight out of the Roman world; like 'uniform' and 'prefect', it was in the vocabulary of the centurions. Theirs was a harsh and unimaginative education and we have inherited it. In the fourth century AD Constantine grafted his decaying Roman civilization onto the vigorous growth of Christianity. The civilization handed down to us was basically Roman, not Christian. Its education was well suited to the training of a prefect élite, people who identified themselves wholeheartedly with their employers, task-masters who got the best results. They were good at memorizing received doctrine and putting it into practice – theirs not to reason why. Unlike the Greeks, they were not encouraged to 'search out curiosities'. Uniformity, getting everybody to march in step, the use of force on children, were characteristics of the Roman world that we have inherited. It is a set-up conducive to the maintenance of an establishment. In an atmosphere where questioning is inhibited, credulity grows.

This is the only way I can find to explain some of the Dickens-like features of our present educational system. For example the importance that the Educational Institute of Scotland gives to corporal punishment. If they were to come out strongly against corporal punishment, and give a lead, it would disappear from Scottish schools in a couple of years. But they do not. Edinburgh Education Committee wanted to stop corporal punishment in primary schools but the Educational Institute opposed them. One difficulty about corporal punishment is that nobody knows how frequently it is used. Alex Eadie, MP for Midlothian, asked a question about it in Parliament. The reply was that they thought its use was decreasing. That may be true. But equally it may be wishful thinking. Nobody really knows. Edinburgh Education Committee proposed that their teachers should log the occasions on which they used the belt. The Educational Institute of Scotland were against keeping a log. Curious some of the reasons they gave for opposing it. A log of corporal punishment, they said, might be a damning dossier against a pupil; it might do him out of a job.

In the Aberdeen branch of the Institute, ninety voted to retain corporal punishment in primary schools, eight or nine to abolish it. There was considerable support in Britain for the Labour Minister of Education's reintroduction of corporal punishment for handicapped children.

These reactions of responsible people – nearly all of them, I imagine, kind, reasonable people – are explicable only on the basis that their own education was narrow and inhibiting and provided them with stock answers which discourage the growth of sympathy and imagination. The establishment had indoctrinated them for its own purposes.

But I think all this is coming to an end. We may be approaching the end of western civilization because I doubt if the prefects of the establishment, educated as they have been, are capable of the imaginative ingenuity and rethinking which could salvage our society. All that many of them can think of is 'more discipline'.

This paper is a plea for less discipline. In our schools we have the fittest generation of children we have ever had in our history. With this fitness has grown a sturdy independence and an equal indifference to sticks and carrots. They believe in the liberty that we only shouted and sang and read about. They need our support and help and are not slow to express their appreciation of it. But if instead of supporting them we try to *discipline*, we will be in trouble.

Now all this is generalization and often I find a broad measure of agreement about the particular instance when I have failed to find it over the generalization. I taught in Germany before the war and the

F

Nazis told me what unattractive characters the Jews were. When I asked if they had known any Jews well, a Nazi family told me that they had Jews as neighbours: 'They were pleasant people, but of course they weren't typical.' In this spirit I put the following particular instance to the disciplinarians.

Peter Hayes was taken away from the school where I work and sent to an approved school in the south of Scotland, because he stole. Why did he steal? I do not know. But I find that when we look into the records of pupils who steal, we generally find an unhappy home background. Peter's parents were divorced. He lived with his mother and his stepfather.

When he returned to us after a year in the approved school, he was a different character. Several teachers said that he was much more difficult to get on with. Previously, although he stole, he was a reasonable, pleasant pupil. Now he was sullen and hostile. I sent for Peter. He was unexpectedly forthcoming. I said that his teachers had told me that he used to be a friendly character in the classroom but now he had changed. 'Yes,' he said, 'that's right.' I asked him why. He said, 'Well, in the approved school, I learned that you had always to back up the others. If somebody cheeked a teacher, you all cheeked the teacher too. It was the thing to do. You get into the way of it.' So now in the classroom here was Peter lined up against the teacher. He had learned in the approved school to accept the indoctrination of his group. The teacher might be OK or not OK, but you were against him. As soon as an argument began, you weighed in against the teacher, added fuel to the flames and sat back and enjoyed the blaze. If you were then sent along to the headmaster, it proved you had played your part.

Peter was caught between two loyalties – loyalty to his group and loyalty to teachers who had treated him with consideration. When he became angry I realized that he was really trying to obscure from himself the truth that he had been less than fair to some of his teachers.

Trouble simmered round about Peter most of the time. He grew his hair very long and became a Rocker. Then one day the trouble which I had always feared erupted. He shouted to a teacher that he was a fucking bastard and he would drive a knife through him. The teacher reported it to me, and Peter agreed with his account of the incident.

I thought that if we could cope with Peter we would begin to understand the problem of delinquency, and so be on the way to solving it. We will never solve it by talking in general terms; we have to consider the particular human being. Slowly I pieced together the background to Peter's outburst. It had started casually enough in the previous class. Peter had been feeling a bit below par anyway and another pupil had been pulling his leg about his long hair. 'A row?' I asked. 'No, no. He's a skinhead but he's a pal o' mine and it wasna really serious, but I got annoyed, and I wasna in a good mood when I went to the next class. Then when the teacher shouted to me to hurry up I said back to him "So?" He got annoyed at that and nudged me and I shouted back at him.'

But the story did not begin with the previous class. At what point does an eruption of this kind really begin? What Peter had not told me, probably had not thought relevant enough to tell me, was supplied by another teacher whom Peter trusts. His mother was in hospital, his stepfather was at sea, and he had sat up for two nights with his dog which was ill. The dog died. The taunting about his long hair had come at a time when his defences were down and his emotional reserves low.

So I say to the traditionalists, 'What do I do with Peter? Discipline him?'

What I did was nothing – apart from talking to him. Without prompting from me, he said that he was sorry about his outburst. I just listened. I did not comment.

The disciplinarians are outraged at this absence of retaliation. 'They get away with murder,' they say angrily. 'There is no discipline in this school.' We have a fair number of pupils, boys and girls, like Peter. One or two of them, I think, if the situation arose and the circumstances were contributory enough, *could* drive a knife through somebody. Come to think of it, doesn't that apply to us all? As Chesterton said in one of his Father Brown stories, the frightening thing about a murder is not that it is something monstrous and alien to our character but that, given the circumstances, *we* might have done it. Part of our job in school is to make it less likely that some pupils, already in trouble, will commit murder. The way to achieve that object is to show them that we care about them and that we love them.

The world is crying out for tenderness, warmth and loving attention. If the educational revolution takes place, this will be its basis — a new care and respect for the human personality, a concern to shelter it and help it grow in freedom. At present the school feels the stresses of the transition from old attitudes and responses to new attitudes. In child guidance clinics and amongst social workers there is a warmth that is often absent from the classroom. Those who work in child guidance clinics beg us to tolerate the delinquents, even though they have made little encouraging response so far to such friendship as has been offered them. Social workers provide a fuller picture of the home circumstances of the delinquents and those teetering on the edge of delinquency, and beg us to go easy on them although they realize how much they are asking of us.

It is more difficult for the teacher in the classroom. He has a curriculum to get through. The wearisome dullness of the curriculum is far more of a strain on pupils and teachers than parents think. A century from now people will read the examination questions with an incredulous smile and wonder why we teachers put up with this nonsense for so long. The teacher is as much the victim of this unintelligent and bankrupt educational system as is the pupil. When the classroom situation becomes intolerable, pupils take to violence or drugs, or run away. Teachers have nervous breakdowns and go to mental hospitals where other prefects of the establishment try to repair them with electric shock treatment and send them back to the front line, to fire at the pupils more questions on the rainfall of Australia, photosynthesis, the Petition of Right, covalent bonds, the exports of Uruguay, the Mason Dixon Line, anodes, Leonardo and Garibaldi and Titus Oates, catalysts, the causes and course of the Thirty Years' War, wavelengths and frequencies, the state of the Scottish Church in 1560, polymers, Euler's Theorem, contractile vacuoles, vitamins, newtons, the Pilgrim Fathers, the present subjunctive of *pouvoir*, and Bonnie Prince Charlie. There is an inhuman Aztec quality in this piling up of huge temples of facts which I believe will perplex future historians, surveying our times. 'Not bread but a stone' is a recurrent pattern in human history, emerging at times when repetitive routines are unintelligently and meticulously observed. Some day psychiatrists will discover what compulsive reflex caused all these classroom confrontations between eager youth and conscientious maturity. The children had so much they needed to learn; the teachers had so much to give. The transaction could have taken place in an atmosphere of warmth and goodwill and cooperation. But most of it was gratuitously dissipated as if by the deliberate intervention of some malevolent and destructive power inducing ill-will on both sides.

Moloch was the god to whom children were sacrificed. Is there some compulsive need in the adult psyche which seeks the suffering of children? Are the colleges and the grammar schools and the comprehensives the modern equivalent of the temples of Moloch? But teachers are equally the victims of this system; they are equally sacrificed on the altar of education.

When I look at this spectacle of waste of life and goodwill, and our apparent inability to avoid it, the pupil shouting curses at the teacher, the teacher exasperated beyond endurance, I begin to wonder if our emancipation from irrational forces, our civilization, has advanced much from the time when the educational system was in the hands of the prophets of Baal. Are we kidding ourselves and being facilely optimistic when we think we can cope with these angers?

But it is in the nature of human life to be optimistic and to go on seeking to diagnose the forces that threaten us and to cope with them adequately. At this level I would suggest that it is within our power to restore harmony between the generations but only if we analyse the situation much more fully. There is a blind yet cunning force called the establishment which throughout history has been deceiving us. The religious system, the educational system, the legal system do not exist for our benefit. They are establishment mechanisms, propaganda machines over which is thrown an aura of mystery and untouchableness, a magic voodoo. The Russians discovered that religion was the opium of the people, and then went ahead to use the educational system to drug its pupils, so to indoctrinate them that they would not question the Russian establishment. Education performs the same function in Moscow, London and Edinburgh; it inhibits questions and maintains the regime. But we retained our reverence for the legal system until the days of the Industrial Relations Act and the thalidomide enquiries. 'What?' thundered the Tory leaders in tones of real or affected awe, 'you do not mean, do you, that you will challenge

THE LAW?' Perhaps for the first time in British history a knowing smile began to curve along the hitherto reverential lips of ordinary people like trade unionists. The law had lost its magic. Another totem had fallen.

This does not mean that all religion is phoney or all law crooked. In the desert of European education there are oases of living water. There are many individual teachers whose lives are spent in helping their pupils to live more fully, who have understood and seen through the establishment mechanism which uses the examination system to prevent the pupils from becoming free. One of the hopeful signs of the present situation is that the number of these teachers is increasing, reinforced by recruits from the ranks of those who only yesterday were themselves teenagers. Maybe there is some substance for believing that we are on the eve of an educational revolution. Teachers of the world, unite. You have nothing to lose but your canes.

Gene Adams

Mark: a case study

His name was Mark, as I very soon discovered. You always find out the names of the trouble makers pretty quickly. He was about twelve, with a charming smile, straight brown hair flopping over his brow and bright blue eyes with a devious look in them. In a group of fifteen children, the presence of one Mark seemed almost immediately to double the numbers.

It was a half-class because the subject was art. The school, though unenlightened in many ways, at least recognized the necessity for halving the class for any lesson which centred around a practical activity. Anyway the room was so small that you could only fit about fifteen into it. The building dated from 1860 – one of the products of the London School Board. Its design was repellently monotonous, with long shiny corridors from which brown-tiled classrooms opened. It was also confusingly intricate because of the elaborate set of separate entrances – the usual late Victorian 'apartheid' of one for boys, one for girls and the other for infants. We were in the infants' room, hence the smallness I suppose, and the easy access to the ugly asphalt playground with its brick wall and locked street gate, and the smelly outdoor lavatories. The year was 1964.

Usually there is a kind of summing up period for a new teacher. It might last one or two lessons of unnatural politeness, after which whatever attitude normally prevails in the class – hostility, apathy or well-motivated eagerness to learn (top stream) – reasserts itself. Mark's class took its cue from him. They did not waste time over an introductory period. He set the tone straight away with an unruly sortie around the room stabbing any unfortunate child who happened to get in his way with a pin, and alternated this activity with spells dedicated to the production of the kind of obscenities to which modelling clay has an unfortunate and natural tendency.

All of this was accompanied by a great deal of hysterical laughter from the other children, helpless with admiration, and punctuated by various four-letter words and much purposeless noise; or purposeless only if one imagines that the purpose of speech is to communicate. Of course after a few years' teaching one begins to realize that speech has other purposes too, for example to provide a kind of noise-barrier against a teacher, who is thus reduced to yelling at top volume, so adding to the row and probably also to the tension and hostility.

Before teaching in a school, I had worked for a few years in a kind of play centre to which the local child guidance clinic used sometimes to direct problem children, so I had a rough idea of the difference between naughty behaviour and what psychologists describe as 'disturbed' behaviour. I felt Mark's behaviour was disturbed and decided to ask for some information about him from the senior staff. To my surprise, there was none. He was uniformly regarded as a pest, but nothing more than that. My tentative mention of the word 'disturbed' brought knowing smiles and polite rebuffs.

Within a matter of days it became clear that Mark was subjecting me to the familiar test. How outrageously could he behave before provoking a strong reaction from me? And what form would my reaction take? He turned up one day with a 'secret' something which he ostentatiously passed round the class, accompanied by delighted sniggers. The shocking object was a contraceptive.

Mark was just about twelve at the time. I supposed that if contraceptives were being passed round the class I ought to take some kind of action. Presumably the children expected me to be shocked and clearly this was 'challenging my authority'. I also imagined the school would expect me to take some kind of action. I was not sure what to do. Should I recommend compulsory sex education, discuss family planning, discipline, manners? It all seemed to be rather pointless, especially as I hardly knew these children. I decided to ask advice from the head.

He was an elderly man in his last few years before retirement. He had spent probationary years in the unbelievable conditions under which London School Board teachers of late and post-

Edwardian period seemed to have worked. Classes of ninety or so were apparently not unheard of, as he never tired of telling us. It was difficult to feel that a mind moulded under such conditions could deal with the problems of today's schools. Nevertheless he had grown up in London, which was more than I had. He even had a broad Cockney accent. Perhaps he could communicate with these tough little kids better than those of us with 'posh' accents, and in my case at least, with memories of a prim c of e school, academically and religiously inclined.

I asked the head if he would have a little chat with Mark. I pointed out that in my opinion caning would not be the right way to deal with him, because Mark's disturbed behaviour was caused by problems of some kind or another.

Next week I noted that Mark was behaving exactly as before – if anything with more open hostility.

'What did the head say to you?' I asked when the other children were out of earshot. 'Dunno,' he said laconically. 'He caned me.' And that was the end of that little dialogue.

Mark was indifferent to caning; it had happened to him so many times before. He was also indifferent to the head. He had now 'placed' me alongside the heads of the world. I had sent him along to 'get the cane'. Just one remove from actually administering it myself, but even less worthy of admiration – or so the reasoning goes.

I was incensed. How dare that old man totally disregard my diffidently stated request. And what contempt in his action for both the child and myself. I made a resolution not to repeat that mistake.

Mark taught me the first lesson for a green teacher: don't rise to a child's challenge. To be occasionally blind or deaf is a most useful and necessary talent. And from the head I had learnt the second lesson of the would-be nonauthoritarian teacher in an authoritarian situation: if you want to remain untainted avoid asking for help.

Of course this is impossible. If the school atmosphere is very tense, the combination of pressure from below by rebelling children, and from above by conforming colleagues, will soon become unbearable. As is well known teachers have a high rate of breakdown. Faced with this all too common situation, the usual response from an inexperienced teacher is to conform to the stereotype policeman-teacher role. Often very young or academically orientated teachers, who probably went to highly authoritarian schools, will actually outdo the domineering attitudes of those above them. If well managed, this can soon lead to promotion! If such teachers are also blesesd with a dominating personality, they will end their probationary period with a glowing comment on the all-important part of the report which deals with 'class management'.

Another common response to this situation is for the teacher to overidentify with the children, sometimes to the extent of practically jettisoning his own adult status. This can be an equally unsatisfactory exercise. After all most children and teenagers regard a person of over twenty-one as definitely past it. They do not have any illusions about the difference between themselves and these aged persons, and can quickly despise a teacher who pretends otherwise. No child can be unaware of his need to depend on adults, and he must have the assurance that the adult is strong enough to depend on. The adult 'in charge' has the paradoxical task of allowing the child his right to be dependent, while simultaneously helping him to assert his evergrowing right to independence, which includes opposition to the teacher himself.

The only path left to the nonauthoritarian teacher is to relate to the children on a person to person basis, making allowances for their youth, but generally expecting them to be reasonably pleasant, honest and cooperative. This is difficult, and in the context of large demoralized classes, sometimes impossible.

It demands inordinate control and maturity from the teacher, combined with a determination to remain relaxed at all costs, no matter how tiring! It also demands a fair amount of cooperation from the children. It can only work in a situation in which individual relationships are not submerged by numbers.

If the school is ultra-authoritarian the head will soon see the non-conforming teacher's 'lax' discipline as a challenge to his own authority. The more personally insecure the head is, the stronger will be his need to force the teacher to conform to his conception of discipline. A school which comes down hard on its pupils, treats the lower rank of its teaching staff with equal contempt. It is all part of the same attitude. The authoritarian is one who 'puts authority above liberty', and moreover who regards authority as synonomous with rank or office, and liberty as something which properly belongs to the powerful, but is occasionally granted (kindly) in small safe parcels to the lesser orders. Faced with the modern attitude that authority is, on the contrary, something which has to be earned, and that it implies mutual respect, conflict is inevitable.

With troubled or disturbed children, the them versus us attitude takes over in inverse proportion to the number of problems the children carry; the mob mentality dominates as soon as the group becomes larger than ten or so, because such is the insecurity of these children that almost any competition for the adult's attention becomes intolerable. And so they retreat into a kind of coagulated group ego, an exercise in mass dog-in-the-manger tactics, united to defeat the teacher if they cannot win the battle to secure his attention individually.

Having learnt that the head would not help me cope with the unruly Mark, I had to decide what could be done. My instinct was to make some constructive collective decision with like-minded colleagues, before calamity struck us all.

One thing I noticed was Mark's tendency (in my classes anyway) to creep into large boxes, to crawl under tables or to perch right on top of a high flight of wall-shelving. I was obviously worried about the possible danger and mentioned it to a friend who had had experience with maladjusted children. I was told that it was quite common for such children to creep into small places – it made them feel more secure. Mark, aged twelve, was behaving the way children of half his age were supposed to when uncertain of themselves.

After that conversation, I decided to let Mark stay under the table or on top of the cupboards. If he was feeling more secure, he would be less trouble. I just hoped he would not fall off, or accidentally electrocute himself. So for the next few weeks, Mark spent his art lessons doing absolutely nothing, sitting on top of about five shelves smiling down upon the rest of us benignly.

I used to keep one wary eye upon him, ready to rush with first aid in case he suddenly came hurtling down, and the other eye upon the door in case of an unexpected visit from the head. I mentally rehearsed the conversation he and I would have, if he did pay us a visit: 'Oh yes, Mark is observing the change in visual angle of the human body when seen from above – a kind of fly's eye-view, in fact. Well, yes, actually I was just going to pass him a drawing board.' Fortunately this never happened.

As my first term wore on, I discovered that I was not alone in my difficulties with Mark and his gang. Without realizing that it was not at all my place to agitate for such radical reforms, I asked for a staff meeting to discuss his problems. This was greeted very coldly. I was informed that the head had abandoned such meetings on problem children *years* ago, because a teacher had become too knowledgeable about certain children, and this had caused embarrassments so severe that they were never explained further than that. I pressed on, nevertheless, impelled by the weekly anxiety of anticipating that particular class.

In the end the meeting was called, but boycotted by the head, and presided over by his deputy, a gentle and pleasant man, an excellent disciplinarian and liked by staff and children equally. This man was often treated with public contempt by the head – one of his great failings apparently being that he refused to cane children who were sent to him for 'discipline'. The systematic humiliation inflicted on him by his superior eventually bore fruit; he took to locking himself away for long periods in his office, and finally left because of a 'breakdown'. When he recovered, he was advised not to return to the strains and stresses of teaching, a sadly familiar story of how some of the best teachers are forever lost to the schools.

At the special meeting, we examined the detention book and discovered that Mark was booked in advance for every single detention period that term. With such a heavy monopoly of his spare time, some inevitably thought that the only other punishment likely to have effect would be the 'infliction of pain' as Plowden has it. But that too was dismissed by Mark as simply another facet of an unpleasant and incomprehensible school situation.

It was decided therefore to ask his parents to come for an interview. This was duly done. His form teacher, who interviewed them together with the head, later described them as 'charming'. The inference was that it was simply incomprehensible how they could have produced such a ghastly brat; they seemed helpless to deal with the situation themselves and it was up to us to stem the tide of delinquency.

Some facts emerged also. Mark was very much younger than his siblings – almost an only child, in effect. Everyone else in the family went out to work. They lived in a high-rise flat where the neighbours insisted on absolute silence from Mark who was never allowed to 'bang things' indoors, and had no recreational facilities. His mother insisted in the face of some disbelief (politely masked no doubt) that he was 'very sensitive'. This was the only part of the interview which did not go down well and was repeated later to loud guffaws in the staffroom.

The end of term arrived and the great report farce came upon us. I had no idea how to approach this ritual – one of the many things our education diploma had not deigned to deal with. In great astonishment I saw the comment of Mark's form teacher, the one person who might feel it a duty to act as advocate for the child however difficult. His progress was described as follows: '*English:* Vicious, obscene and deceitful.' Short, crisp and entirely beside the point.

This was a comment on a twelve year old child by a grown person *in loco parentis*. The report took the form of a little book, a page for each year, intended to be a permanent record of Mark's progress at school. The remark was a good example of a not uncommon abuse of a position of privilege. Apart from this, what kind of comment did the statement make about the impact on Mark of his English lessons?

I had often passed that particular classroom, filled with unnaturally silent children bending over their books copying something off the board. In the open doorway the teacher leaned, bored, keeping an ear open for any signs of trouble in other classrooms. At the first sign of excitement elsewhere she would immediately dash uninvited to the rescue. It is often said that the vast majority of discipline problems are caused by boring lessons, usually referring to bored pupils. Less often does one hear that teachers who are perpetually interfering with the discipline of others and who are heard most often in the staffroom obsessively chewing over this or that confrontation, are all too often bored stiff with teaching. Not only are they totally uninspired by any branch of knowledge, but they are also not interested in people, and therefore have nothing to communicate, not even simple affection.

Time passed and the impasse between the staff and Mark continued to grow. Because of the reinstituted practice of special meetings on problem children, it was no longer possible for teachers to act in isolation with regard to Mark; hence it was no longer possible for him to be totally booked up for detentions as before. Also it was harder to consign him to a beating because there were now about two or three staff (out of about twenty) who vocally opposed it.

I soldiered on, struggling to provide him with something which would appeal to his well-developed destructive instincts and leave the rest of us in peace. Also, more important and much more difficult, I tried to remove him from the limelight which his reputation automatically conferred upon him. For several weeks he was happily occupied with a wood carving. This was a large block of wood, some rather blunt chisels and a large wooden mallet. Joyfully he smashed away at the wood, making a terrible noise and splintery mess, and only occasionally taking a friendly tap at the skull of some passing girl, unwisely walking within mallet's reach.

He spent most of his weekends obsessively watching demolition squads on nearby building sites and told me that his ambition when he left school was to 'smash things up', starting with the school itself of course. It was only too apparent that he had already embarked on a programme of self-training.

I found myself rather liking him – a distinct advantage in the situation, in fact essential. Nothing is more difficult than to be fair to a child who not only behaves repellently but whom you also distinctly dislike, a feeling which is of course immediately returned with interest.

The liking I felt was not shared by most of the staff. His form teacher remained implacable. She was a great believer in the cane and expressed this belief with a defiance which indicated a certain guilt not far below the surface. To question caning was some kind of challenge to her authority. She suspected that any questioning of the ultimate method of punishment must have a hidden motive directed at her personality. Because she was not able to be objective on the subject, she assumed no one else could be either.

As the situation between Mark and the staff deteriorated, I found it as hard to contain his extraordinary behaviour, as to ward off those members of staff who advocated strong-arm methods. In spite of the evidence of the punishment book and his primary school report, both of which indicated a constant use of corporal punishment since at least the age of eight, the notion that a caning would be a last resort continued to be put forward as a solution.

Eventually Mark resolved the crisis in his own inimitable way: he exposed himself at the back of the science class.

The science teacher had the loudest voice in Christendom. One heard the resonant tones bowling down the glassy corridors and wondered if the children had been bludgeoned into some kind of scientific enlightenment, or simply stupified into incipient deafness.

So Mark kindly provided a little extra interest at the back of the class and in the company of a group of giggling girls. The reaction of authority was instantaneous.

'Ah, now we've got him,' declared the head, reaching out for the telephone and dialing the educational psychologist. He had been along to administer a test to Mark some months before, as Mark himself reported, with an amused and cynical twinkle in his eye, saying he had been seen by 'some kind of nut asking me stupid questions'. Since then nothing had been heard from the clinic. It would seem that Mark had now discovered a way to instant psychological treatment. He was sent off to weekly 'tutorials' at the clinic, and he continued to attend these till the end of his school days.

The following year Mark moved out of our orbit. By the time we met again he was a tall gangly fourteen year old. Still a problem; still attending the clinic; still the centre of all kinds of trouble; but with one vital mitigating factor – he had lost his vicious need to hurt others. A small success for the efforts of those of us who insisted on trying to discuss his problems and treat them instead of simply suppressing them, thus building up more and worse for the future.

He left school eventually at fifteen and with absolutely no educational qualifications beyond a minimal literacy, though he was not unintelligent. From time to time we heard reports of him being in trouble and mostly unemployed. All he had in the way of certificates, in a world which places all too much importance on pieces of paper, was that school report, a nasty little document composed of endless indifference, punctuated occasionally by pure bile. What kind of job would that get him?

I had learnt that the position of a teacher who cannot conform with authoritarian precepts of the hierarchy was indeed perilous. The shadow of victimization is everpresent, and is neither pleasant nor conducive to professional confidence. To survive one had to compromise. I had to convince those above that despite eccentric ideas,

I could maintain discipline when required – and also to convince myself and the children that this was indeed so! Children, also great conformists, are quick to spot differences between those in authority, and to work on those differences to their own advantage. It is a great mistake to be sentimental about children – the more they are exploited and oppressed, the quicker they learn to do likewise.

I had to learn that the only real way to cope was to keep enthusiasms alive. All that time spent on extra projects – plays, magazines, exhibitions – paid over and over again, however exhausting.

It was necessary too, to learn to stand my own ground. The head-teacher, usually unconsciously identified as some kind of mother/father figure, is not going to bail out critical or questioning staff. Headteachers are interested primarily in one thing – keeping up appearances. To that end they will sacrifice any person and any principle.

As a nonauthoritarian teacher you will find most of your natural allies are among those of your own rank. Only if you form a stable nucleus of like-minded and supportive colleagues, can you hope to survive these pressures and keep your sanity and your principles more or less intact. You have to learn to be more aware of your own weaknesses so that, given intolerable stresses, you know when and how to retreat until you have regained your strength. You have to be both aware of the danger of using those weaker than yourself – children – as scapegoats, and adept at fending off those higher in the pecking order. You have to realize that your sometimes greater self-awareness does not excuse you from being holier than thou. You have to recognize that there are as many different ways of teaching as there are different people. You have to keep learning – from your colleagues and from your pupils.

The position of the nonauthoritarian teacher from the ranks is at the best a nerve-wracking compromise, and at worst a total impossibility. Those who point the finger at this obsolete system and call for urgent radical reform, are ignored at society's peril. If reasonable and humane voices are ignored, the voices of the Marks of the world will be heard instead.

Rhodes Boyson

Order and purpose

School discipline is the way a school is organized to ensure that the majority of its pupils gain most benefit by absorbing learning, training themselves for adult life and developing their personalities. The type of discipline will depend on the view of scholarship, society and the individual held by the headmaster and staff, bearing in mind the needs and mores of the catchment area.

Schools are part of the preparing ground for the continuance of a civilized society which has itself developed by the efforts of millions of men over thousands of years. Civilized society, like reading and writing, is not a natural development, as sex is, but is something which man has structured for the greater freedom of the vast majority who, like Hobbes, would find that outside its boundaries life is 'solitary, poor, nasty, brutish and short'. Left to himself without the support of preceding generations man would neither read nor write, have little sense of history and the arts and would live a painfully primitive existence in which the weak and sensitive would go to the wall.

I do not believe in the cult of the noble savage nor in its modern equivalent that if you leave man untrammelled by restrictions he will grow up noble, pure, selfless and learned. If there was ever such a time it was in an uncrowded pastoral society and certainly not in the concrete jungles of our cities where to let a child run free is to ensure that he would be run over or fall from the twentieth floor. I accept the fall of man and believe that man is not perfectible in this life, and most humanists would accept that if man is perfectible it would take half a million years to reach that state. Thus the Christian and the true humanist concerned for culture and the happiness of man find themselves allied against the millenarians who believe it is only capitalism or communism or socialism or repressed man or a bunch of politicians preventing us from reaching perfection. Such a view is as illogical and as dangerous as to expect the number of traffic accidents to be decreased by doing away with the rules of the road, policemen, drinking laws and traffic lights.

But it by no means follows that a school has to be obsessed by authority, order, rules and discipline. The more obvious it is to parents and children that a school is meeting the real needs of the young, the less call has to be made to any form of sanctions. Children expect schools to be for schooling – they do not expect them to be a cross between a holiday camp, a play pen and a student talk-in. Working class children in particular want to get on with the job of learning and preparation for what is to them the real life. Unlike many teachers who have gone from school to college and back to school they know that the life outside school is generally more exciting and more real than school can ever be.

This does not mean that school should be unexciting. Man is a tribal animal and Robert Ardrey's (1967) *The Territorial Imperative* and Anthony Jay's (1972) *Corporation Man* show how far primitive genes still condition us. As adults identify with a football club, political party, golf club or working-men's club, boys (and girls) will identify with a successful school. A school should be lively, the teaching should be interesting, there should be a great variety of sport, music and other activities. The relationship between the head and staff, and the staff and children should be courteous and full of respect and confidence. Boys should be proud of their school which should be seen clearly as a competitive institution wishing, within reasoned rules, to win at sport and gain the highest successes for its pupils. School uniform is a sign of belonging and when they don it they show they are joining a school as men put on scarves to identify with their football team.

There is no doubt in my mind that one of the reasons for the 1000 per cent increase in adolescent violence in the last eighteen years is because their schools have failed them in the sense of giving identification, in passing on literacy and numeracy and in preparing them for the society they wish to enter. If the school is not worth identifying with boys will form a thug gang inside the school and march in uniformed colours with scarves and boots to fight and cheer in the crowd of their chosen professional football club. This is what happens when we fail to channel properly the energies of vigorous youngsters. It was fascinating that in the Schools Action Union demonstration in the summer of 1972 the schools which provided most of the 500 marchers were unpopular working class schools with no uniform, and middle class schools where they had given it up. In both cases they were really protesting against a liberation they did not want and were really clamouring for some form of identity.

The generation gap is largely a middle class phenomenon because the parents have fled from their responsibilities. Children are as concerned as ever for the approval of their parents and they will as always push their revolts to test this affection and their standards. The identification of parents with the school is vital if it is to be successful. This does not mean a committee of twenty on a Parent-Teacher Association raising money for a paddling pool or presenting a cheque to the retiring deputy headmaster. It means that parents identify with the aims of the school, that they have regular and easy contact with the staff and that they are involved in helping to run the school's teams and societies. Parents desire identity too and if they find it in the school the problems of residual discipline will be few. At Highbury Grove we see parents twice before their sons enter, there are Parent Associations meeting regularly in all the Houses for social and academic purposes, they help to run the House Clubs, have accompanied school journeys, and are encouraged to come into the school at any time to see the housemasters.

To me the parents and the boys are the consumers of education and the success or failure of Highbury Grove rests not upon the comments of visitors or inspectors but in the continued confidence of parents and boys. The confidence of parents is shown by the heavy oversubscription of boys to enter every year and the confidence of boys by the high attendance (92–94 per cent) in a city-centre area. It is interesting to compare such high oversubscription and attendance with the figures of other schools where boys and parents do not identify with the schools and where the aims and ideals are not those they accept. That at least 6,000 boys in Inner London are playing truant every day, that one in five in Salford schools, one in ten in Liverpool schools and one in eight in Manchester schools have been known to be absent regularly shows the problem of schools in city areas where there is a lack of identity with parents and boys. I sometimes wonder if teachers in these areas do not welcome the absence of troublesome boys to allow the rest to learn without disruption. Certainly the truancy in some areas and schools of a third to a half of the fourth year boys throws doubt on the reasoning behind the raising of the school leaving age.

The 1968 Schools Council enquiry *Young School Leavers* shows clearly how parents and boys in working class areas could be encouraged to identify with schools. Unlike their teachers they regard schools as places which lead them into good jobs. With this in mind the boys rate English, mathematics and technical subjects as the important studies, while girls list domestic science, English and mathematics, an interesting contrast which clearly indicates that most girls see their future as housewives and mothers. Both parents and boys identify schools with learning. This may seem obvious enough yet the collapse of many city-centre schools is probably a result of teachers (encouraged by their education authorities) going there as missionaries to preach a culture and a liberation which has no meaning to the boys and which they spurn by violence and truancy. If teachers would return to the idea of imparting basic skills and preparing children for work and adult life, most of the school problems would disappear. There is no relevance for pupils and parents in continued visits to the monuments of London or in decorating expeditions to old people's homes when they prefer to see Manchester United playing Arsenal, when they themselves are living in overcrowded housing conditions at war with either the council or the private landlord. Any attempt to organize schools with the casual friendliness of youth clubs will fail if only because 60 to 70 per cent choose not to attend youth clubs.

In the well-run cheerful school at peace with its area, disciplinary problems can be minimal. But this is not to deny that problems have increased over the last few years owing to the crisis of authority in our society, the growth of the large school and the diversity in teachers' approach to children. Since the war there has been a continued sniping at lawful authority and just as in certain schools children find nothing to identify with, so in our present-day society many people have ceased to identify. The police, the Church, the politicians are under constant attack and little defence is made. In certain fields we are dangerously near anarchy and it seems that any determined minority group can shake a government and obtain their own wishes. Thus an antiauthoritarian attitude has seeped into school often encouraged by some teachers who do not realize the dangers of their approach.

In March 1972 Eltham Green Comprehensive School in London circulated a report on discipline. This listed three major causes of indiscipline: the variety of standards set by different teachers, the emotional instability of the children and the increased size of schools. The former is very important. If a school is itself divided in its approach to children it will not succeed. Many schools are now a battleground between teachers with a traditional formal approach and those with a progressive informal approach. The sufferers are the children. If instead of local education authorities propagating the myth that all schools are equal they frankly stated that certain schools are traditional while others are progressive, and if teachers were encouraged to go to schools with whose philosophy they agreed, children would know how they stood and we could see which method was the more successful by the number of parents who want their children to join a particular type of school. The colleges of education churning out 'liberal' and 'progressive' if not revolutionary ideas of teaching which they themselves will never be called upon to apply have done untold harm! But at least we can minimize their influence by encouraging teachers with similar views to work together.

I do not really know what is meant by 'emotional instability'. The term can embrace a broad selection of problems – broken homes, mothers of younger children out at work and difficult housing conditions. I always feel, however, that it is a school's job not to look for excuses but to overcome problems. After all, many of us who grew up in poor conditions in the 1930s found in our schools a means of liberating our spirits. Nor do I think that the rapid increase of supportive services of social workers and counsellors is much good: they simply divide authority and provide excuses to pass the buck. Possibly their only function is to reduce unemployment. Children have to be encouraged and taught to fit into society as it is, not be encouraged to keep knocking on someone else's door!

The large school will inevitably increase disciplinary problems.

Staff and children cannot know one another well especially where there is a good deal of specialization. In a huge building where staff and boys are constantly moving around there are difficulties in identifying trouble-makers on corridors (unless the staff carry cameras) and staff are unwilling to risk their classroom discipline by having a corridor confrontation with a boy they do not know. In the smaller school information on boys and methods passes informally over break but in the large school everything has to be specially structured and many staff, let alone boys, feel lost. The large school and difficult housing and behavioural problems in the centre of our large cities have meant that staff generally live away from the areas in which they teach and the sense of community is further lost.

The raising of the school leaving age will increase disciplinary problems. To some boys the school is an academic institution where they never really succeed, while in the world of work they can earn equal salary and success with their more academically able brethren. More compulsory school education will further structure society and create a sense of real failure amongst the failed. You cannot say on one side that people are mature enough to marry at sixteen, and have the vote and serve on juries at eighteen, and yet maintain that they are so immature that they must remain at school until sixteen. Where a boy knows he has a well-paid job or business waiting for him, between the ages of fifteen to sixteen a school can offer to the less academic pupil little apart from loss of self-confidence, boredom, unrest and loss of income. Far better to let boys leave at fourteen provided they reach a satisfactory basic standard while welcoming them back later when they are motivated to take part in full-time education.

But when all this has been said, how does a school cope with boys who are determined to disrupt its purposes? Has one boy in a class of thirty a better right to cause trouble than have the other twenty-nine to learn? Surely orderly children deserve to expect a suitable working atmosphere to exist in schools? Concern for the ninety-nine sheep in the fold has always seemed to me to precede concern for the one who intends wilfully to stray. I have seen children terrified by schoolboy muggings and a whole class with razorblade cuts on their hands to show they have paid their weekly protection money. There will always be a small minority of pupils prepared to make the lives of their fellows a misery and if society does not show that it is stronger, school and society will be a sad place for the rest. If it is sensible to support an ecology lobby to safeguard the environment there is just as much need for a disciplinary lobby to protect the weak, otherwise their social environment will be grim.

Twenty-five years ago it was the bad boy who did not come to school. We are now nearing a situation where it is the good boy who does not come to school because he dare not! Sir Alec Clegg has referred to a decline of school standards with an increase in violence, vandalism, crime and child difficulties. The Institute of Education of London University in its evidence to the James Committee on teacher training wrote: 'There are schools where conditions are such that no teacher, let alone a young and new teacher can be expected to teach.' Whilst in most schools it is still persistent chattering, a disinclination to work, an intended failure to bring books and pens which can disrupt a lesson, this quickly grows into insolence and a threat to order. England is not as far from America's Blackboard Jungle as some people would like to think and the doubt whether local education authorities will support firm action to restrain wreckers daily brings it nearer.

Arson to schools in Miami, Florida cost £384,000 in 1971. At Sacramento, California, an ultrasonic alarm in the shape of a fountain pen has been tested so that teachers can call for help when pupils riot. The New York Board of Education in 1972 spent £2,500,000 in employing an extra 1,200 guards to protect teachers in its 900 schools. In Britain the attack on a teacher in 1972 in Bristol where he was almost killed before his class, the suing of a Birmingham teacher in 1972 for hitting a boy who had kicked him in the stomach and the stabbing of a boy to death in the yard of a London school in 1971 are the tip of the iceberg. Yet the constant pressure by the authorities to get rid of the cane brings some of us to suspect that they are more concerned to win the applause of the trendy than to protect the law abiding and ensure that there is order in the schools. Parents clamour for order in schools while educational advisers and committees undermine it.

The immediate involvement of parents when pupils overstep the mark is essential provided the right relationship has already been established with parents. Where there is damage or destruction there must be some form of compensation. The form of punishment is less important than that there is punishment, both for the sake of the offender and for the deterring of others. No child resents punishment where there are clear and sensible rules for what is and what is not permitted. Indeed courts run by children are likely to be far more repressive than the rule of the average teacher. But to allow a delinquent child to grow up believing he can get away with breaking rules merely encourages the growth of the adult criminal.

Bernice Martin (1971), lecturer in social studies and economics at Bedford College has written that truancy, vandalism and drug taking are a result of excessive freedom and absence of firm discipline in schools using progressive methods. It is interesting in the Eltham Green report that mixed ability classes were listed as more of a cause of disciplinary problems than were streamed classes. Since they make teaching more difficult and can make the academically backward child more aware of his backwardness in every lesson the argument is probably valid.

There will always be the odd pupil who cannot be contained since schools are neither staffed nor equipped to care for really delinquent children. The less successful a school is in creating identity, and the more it is restricted in its disciplinary framework, the more children will have to be removed. In a society which knows its purpose and supports its teachers within this purpose, it is doubtful if one in 200 children needs to be sent to special outward-bound type boarding schools. Where more are removed they are a commentary on the effectiveness of the schools and the education authorities.

Finally it is as well to remind the reader that the good school is identified by a general ethos of pride and confidence. It is more important to reward punctuality than to punish lateness and the best reward is acceptance by the group and school that this is the behaviour required. Otherwise we will have as many behaviour problems as we have psychological agencies and social workers to discover them. The vast majority of boys will grow up normally if treated normally and this means correction when they do wrong. It will be a pity if our woolly ideas of liberation of the self mean that we are less successful in training our young to responsible adulthood than in making schools and society playgrounds for the gangster thugs.

References

ARDREY, R. (1967) *The Territorial Imperative* London: Collins; London: Fontana

JAY, A. (1972) *Corporation Man* London: Cape

MARTIN, B. (1971) Progressive education versus the working classes *Critical Quarterly* 13, 4, 297–322

SCHOOLS COUNCIL (1968) *Young School Leavers* London: HMSO

Michael Duane

The children we deserve

At a quarter past two I was called from my maths class to 'deal with' the class taken by Mrs Swallow. Just before I entered her room I paused to listen. From the room came a confused noise. Some boys – and girls – seemed to be shouting at the tops of their voices; several desk lids were slammed and a chair fell over. A boy was laughing in a harsh, jeering manner. Through this noise I could hear the helpless bleating of Mrs Swallow vainly calling for quiet.

I opened the door. The class went quiet. Two boys who had been scuffling in a corner at the front of the room stopped and then moved in a shamefaced manner to their desks. Near the window a boy and a girl who had been standing up and fighting over a book, stopped and sat down. The book now lay on the desk with the cover torn off. Five or six boys and girls near the back of the room who had been quietly reading comics looked up at the unusual hush and hurriedly put their comics away.

'I've come to look at the work you've been doing.'

There was an immediate bustle among the many who had not already got their books open on the desks.

'Please, Ma'am, I haven't got a book.'

'Where's the one I gave you at the beginning of the lesson?'

'I don't know, Ma'am. It was on my desk a minute ago.'

'Well, find it or look at your neighbour's book.'

A boy from the back called out, 'Ma'am, I haven't got my exercise book.'

'What have you done with it?'

'You didn't give it back to me with the others.'

'Are you sure you handed it in at the end of the last lesson?'

'Yes, Ma'am, positive.'

'Here's a piece of paper. Work on that for now.'

Other complaints of lost pens, missing pages, lost or damaged books, lack of ink, continued while I toured the room looking at the work. Half a dozen books were reasonably neat and legible. Four children had no exercise books at all and claimed that they had been handed in at the end of the previous lesson. Of the rest nearly all had blots of ink, were scribbled in pencil or had pages torn out. In all the books the work had begun well and then rapidly petered out. By the end of the lesson ten minutes' work had been done under reasonably orderly conditions. I told the class to report to me in that room at four o'clock so that the work could be completed. Some of the class looked very aggrieved.

At four o'clock Mrs Swallow and I waited as the class arrived. Four were missing and would have to be seen next morning. By looking rapidly through the books it was possible to see those who had made some attempt to get work done and to dismiss them at once. Later, as the others left the room, Patrick said, in a voice obviously intended to reach me, 'If only she would keep us in order we wouldn't have to stay in. Others teachers do it, why can't she? It's not fair.' This was not the time to pursue the matter so I asked him to see me in the morning. Mrs Swallow had to collect her baby from the woman who looked after it during the day and could not stay to discuss the situation. She agreed to see me in the morning.

I could guess what would be said. Mrs Swallow would complain that the class would not obey her. That was true. I had seen her at work on a number of occasions, at her own request, so that she could get her lessons started in peace. But even with quite amenable classes she seemed to be unable to plan a lesson that would sustain their interest. The more she nagged at them to listen carefully, the less they heard. She had little coherent theory or skill in making the practice fit the theory. She would grind relentlessly through the exercises in face of mounting resentment and disorder. Her marking was as slipshod as her appearance.

I had tried to get her moved to a school where she might find the work and the children more to her taste. The District Inspector would not agree, though he had in fact, as I discovered later, moved her from another school to ours at the insistence of her previous head-mistress who regarded Mrs Swallow as incompetent beyond remedy. The Inspector assured me that on compassionate grounds the Committee would not hear of another move. That would be tantamount to a request for dismissal and would require very strong evidence to back it up. Mrs Swallow was, in any case, a close friend of the local Union secretary and could rely, therefore, on strong support if she needed it.

I suggested to her that she try a different approach – games, songs, dramatic work. . . .

'I've tried all that before. They just will not work. They are not interested and they are determined not to be interested. I just don't know what to do with them.'

I tried to get her on to a refresher course. She refused because of the difficulty of having the baby cared for in her absence. I got the impression that she really could not be bothered. So, the only solution was for me to resume the practice of being present as often as possible when she started her lessons, even though I realized that the more she relied on me or other colleagues to help her in this way, the more difficult it would be for her to gain the confidence and affection of her classes.

Mrs Swallow was burdened by her youthful marriage to a manual worker with whom she had in common only a burning devotion to left-wing politics. Her husband was a dour, uncommunicative and introverted man, seeing the woman's place in the home and resenting her intellectual friends and her independence. The sagging of her marriage into a state of ill-concealed frustration and hostility made her neglect herself and the flat so that there developed a spiral of increasing irritation with the home and with one another.

During her two years at college she had not been trained to be able to take stock of herself. She had not been helped to gain greater insight into her own and her husband's expectations for the marriage. If she had had this insight she might have been able to build up his confidence in himself and thus lessened his feeling of intellectual inferiority. She had not been trained, through working with children, to understand how they learn and she could not, as a result, build her own lessons round events in their daily lives. In spite of her left-wing sympathies she could not understand that one of the most important things she should do was to get to know the parents of her children and the circumstances in their lives that made them what they were. She had no feeling for education as a joyful experience of extending knowledge and skill.

Her college had failed to teach her that discipline is as much concerned with what has gone on in the family and the neighbourhood *before* the child even starts school as it is with what takes place in the classroom; that four out of every five children in secondary day schools spend only 23 per cent of their waking hours in lessons and that 77 per cent of their sensory impressions, their linguistic experience and their social values must therefore come from the family and the neighbourhood. She had not been taught that where children are indifferent or hostile to school they will be unlikely to take what the school offers to them. She had learnt, as so many young teachers still learn in their colleges, that the child is, somehow, an organism totally isolated from the living matrix of his culture and capable of being moulded in whatever ways the school thinks desirable.

With Patrick the first problem was to keep the discussion away from his particular grievances about Mrs Swallow.

'She can't keep her class in order.'

'How old are you, Patrick?'

'Thirteen and a half, sir.'

'Do you really think that at your age you need somebody all the time to make you behave sensibly?'

'No. But when the others muck about so much you can't help getting mixed up in it sometimes.'

On his own, Patrick responded on a mature level. He would agree, as did the whole class when they were calm, that their 'mucking about' was a waste of their own time as well as that of the teacher, but what came clearly through was their resentment of any teacher (paid for her work, it should be remembered) who had neither the integrity, maturity nor the self-discipline to put her personal worries, attitudes, grievances or convenience second to the needs of the pupils.

Patrick was an intelligent boy, but what resources of personal ambition did he possess that would enable him, or any child of his age, to hold out day after day, against the general climate of attitude and behaviour in the class, the school and the neighbourhood? The school was in the heart of a depressed area with a mixed racial population, high levels of crime and unemployment. Families had little hope that their children, even if they succeeded in school, would get the well-paid and secure jobs they wanted. There was, therefore, an air of fatality, almost of resignation to their lot, that their fathers and mothers had known. They lived either in slums condemned many years before, or in high-rise flats that had broken up what little community feeling had existed in the close and neglected streets. Had the parents been educated to want the privacy, the opportunities for play, hobbies or cultural pursuits like music, art or reading that teachers assume to be essential to family life, they could not provide them for their children. Since the parents themselves worked in dull, monotonous and often dirty work and had little responsibility for their part in that work, they had no experience of the kinds of communication that teachers, lawyers, artists and other professionals take for granted. So their children were not brought up to discuss ideas round the table or to satisfy their curiosity by questions to their parents. Then, as now, there is a clash between what the children and their families expect, on the one hand, and what the teachers, the schools, the inspectors and the whole system of examinations in the competitive ethos of the middle class demands on the other. This clash creates the conditions for bad discipline.

To define what we mean by 'discipline' is certainly not easy. Teachers can more readily quote examples of 'indiscipline'. The following examples have been given to me by teachers in a wide variety of schools within the last two years: Fighting, bullying, extorting money by threats, wearing 'bovver' boots, wearing 'skinhead' hair style and clothes, wearing hair too long (boys) or too short (girls), wearing jewellery in school, not wearing school uniform, eating ice cream or smoking while wearing school uniform, smoking in school, playing cards, gambling, stealing, whistling or shouting in the corridor, running in the corridor, failing to keep to the left in corridors or on stairways, sliding down banisters, 'rude' play between boys and girls, carving names on desks, writing with spirit pens on walls, truanting from school, leaving school without permission during the lunch hour, remaining in the school building without permission during the lunch hour or in the morning or afternoon break, talking in class without permission, reading comics in class, eating sweets in class, failing to write name on completed work, working in pencil rather than in ink and so on.

These offences were punished in a variety of ways. For 'extorting money by threats' (the sum under question was 3p) the police were called into the school. For the other offences the punishment varied from suspension for an undefined period or caning to 'lines', detention after school to do extra work, or public or private rebuke.

When they are asked what they mean by 'discipline' teachers tend to say things like, 'being clean and punctual', 'working hard', 'not getting into trouble', 'keeping his nose clean', 'not wasting time on girls, pop or youth clubs', 'putting first things first' – i.e. getting good GCE results. For the less academically clever pupils, 'steering clear of trouble with the police', 'not wasting money on cigarettes'. Less often they associate the word with religious belief or 'belonging to a church'.

What becomes clear to anyone who has worked in different schools is that the standards of behaviour expected from the pupils vary widely according to the neighbourhood, the type and tradition of the school, the social background of the teachers and what they themselves expect to achieve, the social background and expectations of the parents, the personality of the headteacher, and so on. The behaviour, language and personal relationships that would be held to be normal in private progressive schools such as Summerhill, Kilquhanity, Monkton Wyld or Dartington would be the objects of outraged attack in traditional grammar schools, just as the accepted forms of dress, language and relations in those schools would be the objects of amazed disbelief and ribald comment in the progressive schools. Similarly the more open relationships between staff and pupils now accepted in public schools such as Marlborough would be frowned upon in state grammar schools which have sought to model themselves on what they fondly believe to be 'the public school image'.

Just before the war, as part of my teacher training in the University of London Institute of Education, I did my teaching practice in Dame Alice Owen's Boys' School, a well-known grammar school reputed to owe its origin to the fact that Dame Alice, while milking a cow, had been shot through the hat by an arrow from the nearby Finsbury Butts where newly recruited archers were being trained. She persuaded her wealthy husband, a member of the Brewers' Company, to found a school in thanksgiving for her preservation. To this day the school badge includes crossed arrows and beer barrels rampant, and once a year the boys receive beer money.

My teaching practice consisted in watching 'skilled' practitioners at work – mostly a process of dictating lengthy notes that had to be taken down and written up neatly for homework. Gradually I was allowed to try my hand at teaching. This was easy enough while the master remained in the room, but quite different when he had left. As the door shut behind him the boys would visibly relax, slump back in their seats and prepare to enjoy the session. Why, in God's name, I would ask myself, can they not simply respond to me as they do to old Plumbum, the nickname of the departing teacher? I would start on the lines of my carefully prepared notes, making sure that the boys 'received different types of stimulation', 'alternating periods of oral work with periods of written work', 'using diagrams and drawings (in those days films and filmstrips were rare and often despised in grammar schools) as well as the spoken and written word' – and yet the boys would not be silent or attend as they had done only minutes before. They would fidget, talk among themselves, complain that there was no ink in the inkwells or that their pens were suddenly and unaccountably useless for writing, that their textbooks or notebooks had mysteriously disappeared.

During the question and answer sessions – my training, based firmly on the educational philosophy of John Dewey and on Freud's psychology, had impressed the importance of following up the boys' real interests – I found that the questions would more and more veer away from the subject of the lesson and on to more personal lines about myself, why I wanted to be a teacher, what I thought of the school and, in particular, of the head. Fighting off such improper attempts to erode my 'professional etiquette' by discussing my colleagues with pupils I would steer, cajole or bellow my way back to the main topic. When my tutor visited the school to see me teach I was amazed at the reaction of the boys. They were well-behaved, silent unless questioned, bright-eyed and intelligent in their replies – rather like the boys in *Unman, Wittering and Zigo* whenever the headmaster descended on their unfortunate teacher-victim. I felt moved, grateful for their cooperation, impressed by their ability to sum up so rapidly the situation and relieved that, despite my inadequate performance as a teacher, they had 'taken my side' in the test. At the end of the summer term the headmaster, a clergyman, invited me to join the staff. I did so, sooner than expected, because the school was evacuated to Bedford under the threat of war.

In Bedford we shared the buildings of the Bedford Modern School, a minor public school. For a time we could work for only half a day. For the remainder of that early and fine autumn we spent much time with the boys out of doors and, borrowing some boats from our host school, the maths master and I taught the boys to row. We filled long, strenuous but happy hours on the River Ouse coaxing groups of clumsy boys to that first moment when the unexpected spring and glide of a well-timed stroke tells you that eight individuals have become a crew.

Later that term, after we had passed through the chaos of settling boys and staff in their digs and sorted out the frictions that came from thrusting several hundred lively London boys into the quiet of a rural and rather narrow town community, I became aware that some of the older teachers were critical of my teaching methods and of my relations with the boys. Their reaction was typified by a comment made in a very loud voice as I entered the Common Room for a cup of tea: 'Oh, Duane! I was about to enter your room a few moments ago to quell a riot when I saw that *you* were there!' To which the only reply could be a cool – or seemingly cool – 'Oh, really!' and the private thought, 'You vicious old bastard! The kids wouldn't be as noisy as they are if you lot treated them as human beings or had the faintest idea of what good teaching means.' We had not, in those days, been able to go very far into the roots of 'indiscipline'. The Bernsteins of today were still themselves at school.

Later that term I was summoned by the senior master to his digs for coffee and a rebuke for 'seeking popularity with the boys', and shortly afterwards the rebuke came from the new headmaster (a very 'religious' man with a strong moral conscience who later died an alcoholic) that I was 'engaging in subversive actitivies' by belonging to the Left Book Club and, in particular, by taking a part in a play called *Waiting for Lefty*. He and many of his older staff were deeply disturbed by what they clearly felt to be a 'breakdown in discipline'. The younger staff were swimming, picnicking, playing with the boys and, with the older sixth formers, talking about the war and, occasionally, drinking. The boys, away from home and with fathers in

H

the Forces, were anxious about their families in London, often home-
sick and needing the personal contacts with staff that a boarding
school should, but rarely does, provide.

It would have been difficult, even if it had been either desirable
or possible, to maintain the rigid structures of discipline and the
formal relationships on which the school prided itself in London. It
soon became clear, in fact, that as a result of the more informal
contacts made that autumn discipline in the classroom was becoming
easier. Boys were more cooperative, anxious to spend time with any
teacher who would talk to them or help them with their homework.
I found my own classes quieter and more relaxed. What I had learned
in my training year at the Institute now seemed to have more relevance. There was more community feeling between the boys and the
staff, or at least the younger staff. Driven together by the reluctance
of the local people fully to accept us, we shared our pleasures and
our anxieties as people tend to do when they live together. The rituals
of the classroom were becoming less important because they were
no longer our only points of contact with the boys.

All too soon new premises were found and we resumed full-time
schooling. We began to lose the camaraderie that had grown in that
Indian summer and reverted to the exam-burdened pattern of
'normal' school. The boys were at last being more fully accepted into
the families with whom they lived; teachers' wives and families were
arriving and settling down so that the teachers themselves had more
to occupy them outside teaching hours. Young staff began to disappear from school as they joined the Forces and local women
teachers were recruited in their place, women who had not shared our
experiences and who seemed to need the more formal relationships to
which they had been accustomed in the local schools.

Looking back on the early halcyon period I can see that the discipline was improving because, in some respects at least, it began to
have some of the features of the more relaxed forms of discipline
that I associate with Summerhill. The conditions under which we
were living resembled many of the details of the community life of
that school. Central to the change was the fact that school itself was
not the only reason for personal contacts between boys and staff. The
staff began to be seen by the boys as something like substitute fathers.
Nearly all the staff responded to the needs of the boys for activity

and companionship by cultivating allotments, producing plays, supervising games and simply talking to the boys. They stood to the boys *in loco parentis* as never before or probably since. From the few contacts that I renewed with some of the staff after the war I found that this period was felt by them to be critical to their revaluation of the purposes of education.

Below these obvious factors in the improved relationships was, of course, the substratum, momentarily obscured by the stress of evacuation, of the common social and academic purposes that make a grammar school what it is – the ambitions of the boys, or at least of their parents, to remain in or to reach middle class patterns of living, and the missionary zeal of the teachers to maintain those standards and to extend them to working class boys in the school. And behind all this was the fact that, somehow or other, the whole nation was coming together in the face of a threat to its very survival – or so most people saw it. It was clear that not only was conscription shortly to be enforced but that food and clothing would have to be rationed. Rich and poor were to share the benefits as well as the dangers. Could it be that the war was going to bring us to the verge of something approaching real democracy? That was how some, at least, of the younger staff saw it. The time of disillusion had not yet set in.

Perhaps we may define the discipline of a school as being 'good' when teachers find that they enjoy and are stimulated by what they do; when the children are growing strong and vigorous; when they are learning fast and well what they themselves want to learn; when they are reaching new levels of sensitivity about themselves and others; when the parents see the school staff as colleagues; when they and other local people feel that the school is theirs in a very full sense of use and regard. Discipline is 'bad' when there is a cleavage between school and community; when teachers dislike or feel uninterested in their work; when pupils attend school only because they are forced to; when problems of discipline are always to the forefront of staffroom discussions; when the teachers' talk is peppered by the word and by examples of misdemeanours; when the teachers refer to the parents as people of an inferior culture or having lower standards than themselves; when they call parents into the school only in times of trouble.

Where discipline is good it is because both staff and children are deeply preoccupied and happy in their work and because the work has purpose for them. It does not mean that instances of indiscipline do not occur, but they are seen in perspective as something to be looked at and dealt with rationally. They do not distort the attitudes and the relations within the school.

Teachers are selected, in the main, from the middle class while the majority of their pupils come from the working class. It is not surprising, therefore, that teachers trained in conventional ways find more disciplinary difficulties in 'downtown' schools than in schools with more middle class pupils, even though this situation is itself changing as middle class pupils realize the nature of the society for which they are being prepared, a society demanding even more conformity and less initiative in work. Teachers trained to understand the cultural and social roots of interest, motivation, and love of learning (as were those students who worked with Graham Owens in Trent Polytechnic), see indiscipline not as a personal affront to their own dignity or a threat to the organization of the school, but as a failure of the school to respect the child, his home and his culture, and the failure of a nominally democratic and Christian country to love – i.e. to provide everything needed for a healthy, intelligent and rational adult – *all* its citizens and, especially, *all* its children.

Good discipline results, in any sphere, when everyone concerned is engaged in doing something that he wants to do, using methods that he accepts as suitable to the task and for purposes that are his own or with which he identifies closely. An orchestra displays good discipline (sensitive and harmonious unity) when the individual instrumentalists and the conductor have worked through to the point when they all agree about the particular interpretation to be put on the work to be played. They are all there, in the first instance, because each one enjoys music, wants to play in the orchestra and has been prepared to practise in order to reach what he hopes will be his peak of perfection.

Within the school such a fruitful combination of factors is rarely achieved. Too often the pupils are in school because the law requires them to be, when they much prefer to be at home or playing with their friends. But their dissatisfaction with school may itself spring from several causes. The school may not believe that children should enjoy school and may, therefore, do little to make schoolwork interesting. Or the children's home background is at odds with what the teachers aim to do and there is an atmosphere of conflict always present – either overt in violence, truancy, lateness, slovenly work, bad manners or open indifference; or disguised in the form of boredom and apathy, in a joyless acceptance of rules and in a lack of cooperation evinced, in times of trouble, by lies and evasion.

This latter cause – the discrepancy between the culture of the children and the culture of the teacher – seems to be the most common cause of indiscipline in this country. Basil Bernstein's (1967, 1971) researches into language and its relationship to social class are especially apt for the understanding of the causes of indiscipline in school. School is, above all, concerned with the extension of children's powers of expression and comprehension in language. It is, of course, concerned with other things too, such as health, physical well-being and sensory discrimination, but even these are, at least traditionally, associated with language. But since language is the most sensitive index of differences in culture because it has the effect, for the individual, both of expressing and of reinforcing that culture, any differences in culture between teachers and pupils will be constantly exposed in teaching. Whenever words are being used values are being expressed.

If the teachers like the children and understand and sympathize with their culture, then they will use language to 'bridge the gap'. If, however, they look down on the children's culture (and this will happen especially when the teacher is 'on the way up' from a working class background) the hostility will become obvious to the children, not only through language but through all the more subtle expressions of feeling conveyed in body tensions and other nonverbal accompaniments of speech. Part of the culture is seen in attitudes to school and to education. For many working class families, especially those whose work is unskilled or semiskilled manual labour, school has been experienced as something with little or no relevance to work. You can be an effective caretaker, dustman, lorry driver or building labourer without having learnt how to write a paragraph, solve an algebraic equation or understand the significance of contour lines. The capacity to speak, to count your change or to catch the right bus or train can be picked up out of school.

Further, since the curricula of most schools are heavily dominated by exams or tests with much emphasis on language or the other forms of symbolic expression, middle class children (brought up from birth to use language in a wide variety of ways because such uses of language are the very tools of the middle class in directing, regulating and controlling our complex economy) will succeed in school work because they find the assumptions of school – a middle class institution – similar to those of their home. Working class children, on the other hand, will more often find the expectations of school alien to them and to the assumptions of home and neighbourhood. They will, time and time again, 'fail' and, through the system of marks, gradings and streaming, be *seen* to fail by everyone in the school. The psychological effect of school will, therefore, be to inculcate a sense of failure in the working class child and to erode any natural confidence in himself and his ability. The political effects of such continued conditioning to accept himself as inferior are indeed far-reaching. Centrally there emerges a reluctance to question authority except when despair compels militant action and, when such action is at last undertaken, a readily-aroused sense of guilt, as witness the discomfiture of so many working class speakers during the power strike when assailed by allegations (almost entirely fictitious) that old people had died of cold and patients died on the operating table for lack of electrical power.

Within the school situation itself the effect of repeated failure is to alienate the child from the school and, ultimately, from the notion of education. We see, in evidence of this, that the mass of working class children leave school at the first available opportunity and *never undertake even part-time further education*. This, of course, contradicts the expressed intentions of all governments since 1870, but the continued low level of education of the working class and their consequent inability and disinclination to assume a full share in the control and running of the country very conveniently fits into the central thesis of capitalist forms of production, *viz.* that profit is the main index of efficiency; that profit is maximized when wage levels are minimized; that the ruling class are entitled to more wealth and leisure than the working class, and that, in addition, they are born to be the rulers and to make all the important decisions affecting the lives of *everyone*. We can, therefore, no longer be persuaded that ignorance, illiteracy, poor intelligence, idleness and crime are obstinate characteristics of the working class which time is gradually eliminating. We now see them as inseparable from the very functioning of a class-divided society and built in to the character structure of its citizens by current forms of family upbringing and current forms of formal education.

References

BERNSTEIN, B. (1967) Open school, open society? *New Society* 14th September

BERNSTEIN, B. (1971) *Class Codes and Control* London: Routledge and Kegan Paul

CALTHROP, K. and OWEN, G. (1971) (eds) *Teachers for Tomorrow: Diverse and Radical Views about Teacher Education* London: Heinemann

JACKSON, B. and MARSDEN, D. (1962) *Education and the Working Class* London: Routledge and Kegan Paul

NEILL, A. S. (1962) *Summerhill* London: Gollancz; Harmondsworth: Penguin

Jack Reynard

Downtown school

In an area of vice and desperate deprivation, with all the external signs of indiscipline, and excesses of the worst kinds accepted by society and observed by the children, the school has a compensatory part to play in the formation of moral and spiritual values, in addition to its dual roles of academic and social education. If the school cannot, or will not, accept this challenge, what agency will? If the school does not possess an internal discipline, does not somehow lead its children into sensible discussion and evaluation of the problems, and the by-products of years of neglect, how can these children grow in a near normal way? The school has a key role to play: not the only role by any means (after all, the children are in school for only some six hours a day), but a really vital one.

The school in which I teach is a junior mixed and infant school, which includes a nursery class, and is made up of the hotchpotch of buildings which appear to have been the common legacy of downtown schools throughout the country. The oldest part, adjoining a care-taker's house, was initially built as a kind of YMCA attached to the church, and is due to be replaced in the next few years. The main part of the school is in the shape of the letter F. The lower level is occupied by three infant classes and the upper part by four junior classes. All rooms on both floors are interconnected, but without corridors. A hall built some five years ago adjoins the building and is connected to it by means of a passage; and completely separated in its own grounds is the nursery class built a year ago. This complex layout adds to the problems of the organization of the school and personal discipline.

The area the school serves consists of rundown, multilet, large houses with a great proportion of shared facilities and overcrowding. It is a multiracial school, with ten differing races represented, yet with only a few of the attendant language problems. There are 229 children on roll, of whom forty attend the nursery class part-time. Some parents live apparently normal lives, despite harrowing surroundings, but many are bowed with adversity; many are alone and yet have to support a family; some are intolerably sick yet trying to maintain a crumbling family structure; some families have been completely broken by one or other of the parents' desertion, and yet, despite all these factors, most attempt to care for and rear their children, although success varies to a very marked degree. In general, the parents tend to be hard disciplinarians, yet they neglect cuts, bruises and small details of general care and welfare. They give the impression they want to help, but conditions and circumstances prevent them from knowing how or when to act for the best. As an example of the difficulties facing some parents and their reactions, let me cite the case of Mrs x, a white woman married to a Somali sailor who has three children. She runs a lodging house for Somalis but has contracted a crippling disease which has made her progressively less mobile. This, allied to her husband's absences, means that each child has presented her with increasingly difficult problems. Offered a hospital bed four years ago, she refused because she feared the break up of the family if she accepted. At this moment, two of her children are in hostels, and the youngest child (aged nine) has taken to staying away from home for two days at a time. The vortex of fate has been apparent for a long time and yet society seems so helpless in solving problems such as these at an early enough stage. To this particular brand of self-imposed martyrdom, the school must remain tolerant, yet seek persistently in every way short of direction, to assist the particular child in such need of care and stability.

The following generalizations can be made about the children attending the school: they are well clad and well nourished; they are very excitable (a windy day – a problem in most schools – can be near to a disaster area here); they are easily distracted, have a limited attention span and can 'turn off' at will. (I believe many of their reactions are directly attributable to overcrowded housing conditions.) It has been estimated by the staff that in some years as many as

50 per cent of the intake at five years are emotionally disturbed.

The responsible posts are held by experienced teachers appointed by the managers; the younger teachers have, in the main, been sent as supply teachers or probationers by the LEA, have appreciated the problems and have been happy to stay and work in difficult conditions. Then there are the auxiliary staff of the school who are drawn from a wide area. Their aims are, quite simply, to learn to live together in understanding and tolerance and to give children a stable learning environment; in other words to be a normal school operating in abnormal conditions. To achieve this, the life of the school must be based on mutual respect for all its members and understanding of the difficulties and problems they face. There must be an awareness and appreciation of the progress and success (however slight) gained by each individual within the framework of the school community. Discipline is the catalyst by which all these ideals become possible.

The headteacher has ultimate responsibility for the whole area of working relations within the school community. His ear must be attuned to catch the slightest discord and he must possess the personality, the trust, the respect and the resources to seek the cause immediately and rectify it. The head must be seen to be all things to all people. He must be lonely, as well as sociable; distant, as well as friendly; ruthless, as well as gentle. He must be aware of all that happens within the school confines and outside the school walls to any of his charges and, above all, at all times must be fair and just in everyday matters. There can be nothing flabby or dewy eyed in his relationships. Mutual affection, understanding and respect have never flourished where disorder, slackness and chaos reign.

In my school I try to be a sympathetic and understanding listener; a buffer between differing parties; an upholder of social and academic standards; and, not least, a social adviser for parents and families in need. The head's door must never be closed to anyone, child, parent or staff member, and I must be prepared to listen at any time to apparently trivial details which are, of course, of vital importance to the complainant. This does, on occasion, lead to difficulties, especially when a parent wants an eyeball to eyeball confrontation with a staff member. If there is a complaint from a parent, I insist that I see the parent first and, having gained their view of the problem, I then present the school's view of the incident before there is any question of them meeting the teacher concerned. This cannot be said to be a perfect solution, but it usually works successfully.

The staff are aware of their responsibilities in school routine, and this is made clear to all newcomers to the school in a leaflet presented to them on arrival. School rules are kept to a minimum and are clearly explained to the children. New rules are added only when the staff decide they are necessary and practicable. Each teacher as a member of a team has to be aware of the general behavioural standards of the school and to this end, regular meetings of staff occur (with the head absent). In these meetings, policy is suggested by the whole staff for my consideration. Thus, a generally agreed routine is formulated, and all adhere to this in relation to school organization. Either my deputy or myself supervise all meals which we feel helps to maintain the stability of the school throughout the day.

If bad behaviour outside the school is reported to me, I make a point of talking to the child concerned. I am confident that if we are learning to live together sensibly then every interrelated aspect of our lives must be open to discussion. At least twice or three times a week, I make it my business to walk round the trouble spots of the school. These are sites which, because of the geographical difficulties, tend to be areas where behavioural difficulties can arise. On these walks, I try to take note of breakages of materials, omissions or irregularities in behaviour, and then deal with them accordingly. Wherever I am, and whatever I may be doing, I believe that wrongdoing must be dealt with and poor standards condemned. I must, and do, fully praise hard effort, progress, honesty and social behaviour at every opportunity. As part of this effort, the staff assist by having a weekly 'Good Work' display. Everyone who has done a commendable piece of school work or behaved in an exemplary way is praised publicly, and we see to it that the honours go round as far as is possible.

Standards of performance within the classroom remain by and large the everyday province of the class teacher but I feel I must, on occasion, be able to assess the work. This I do by flitting visits to the classroom, and by regular teaching periods with each class. Another way of maintaining standards is to send all completed work and exercise books home, with a suitable comment by the class teacher and myself on the last page of the book, and with a space left for parental comment.

As leader of a working team, if extra effort is needed in matters such as holiday schools, camps, extracurricular activities, and social events, I must be prepared to give more, to work harder, to make any experiment succeed. I should arrive earlier, leave later and in all do more than any other member of staff, for without such an example of work rate, diffidence soon appears. Society itself has placed the teachers in the position of the last defender of some social virtues, and I know that in this exposed position, professionals look to the head for a lead, even in the mode of punishment within the school. I have used corporal punishment rarely and never without a great inquest as to the cause and effect on the individual child, and no other teacher has to use corporal punishment within the school.

Teachers' discipline must first be self-imposed, and then passed on and reflected in their respect and attitude towards the children, and thence the community. This self-discipline might be called professionalism, and has to be strong enough to survive in poor environments. Many teachers work in conditions which would daunt the most deprived industrial workers. It has to be sustained over very large periods of intense effort, so necessary to stimulate and gain a suitable response from the children. It must embrace high standards as initial aims, but withstand disappointing results. In addition to all the pressures from within the schools, the female teacher working in our area has to undergo the indignity of being accosted by 'kerb crawlers' on their way to and from school (one young girl from a secure village community in north Wales was subjected to this ordeal three times in a journey of 200 yards).

The staff has to work harder to preserve equipment and books, and yet always to encourage their fullest use, knowing full well the limiting background of the children. They are asked always to attempt to maintain social and academic standards, and persistently lift them a little at a time. They are thus asked to be the finest possible exponents of the teacher's art, yet have to work in some of the worst conditions. Little wonder that I am full of admiration for the dedicated band of professionals with whom I am associated and without whose self-discipline the school would collapse. The staff's constant encouragement and understanding bring out the best points of their charges.

Many of the facets of the downtown teacher are mirrored in the auxiliary workers of the school: the caretaker and his wife who provide a breakfast for some early arrivals, pushed out with little food; the 'lollipop man' who shares his lunch hour with the children and says they have taught him the joy of living again; the school secretary who is a real Girl Friday to all the children. As well as these particular individuals, the teaching auxiliary, the supervisory assistants, the kitchen staff and cleaning staff – all are asked to be an individual in a team caring for specific needs of the children and playing their part in the maintenance of a happy social environment. External visitors too play no mean part in the school. The nurse and the welfare officer are constant visitors, know all the children and, in most ways, are the true arrowheads of help and understanding, moving out freely into the homes. Our children must depend on adults for their moral standards, and from each one of this team of workers comes the vital factors of stability, understanding and affection.

So far, I have dwelt on the interrelation between the staff and the children, for I believe the well-being of the youngsters must override all other considerations. But what of the effect of the school's attitude to parental involvement? As an initial member-school of the Liverpool EPA Project, a number of experiments occurred in the school, and they have served to throw some light on parental reactions to entering and being involved in the school environment. During the three years of the scheme, there were positive efforts made to involve parents in the working environment of the classroom. Initially, the move was viewed with concern, but our fears were needless; parents came and went freely, gaining confidence all the time. From these experiments, both parents and staff have come to realize more of each other's problems, and have been more ready to understand each other's point of view, especially as parents began to pour out individual difficulties in domestic and child relations more readily. In addition, through well-presented publications and displays around the district in various shops and centres, the aims of the school and its philosophy began to be more appreciated by the parents, and on the school side, as we began to mix and express ourselves more freely together, we started to appreciate the depth of some of the problems which were clouding the lives of some parents, and thus affecting the children's responses. Parents helped willingly in after-school clubs, involving

119

swimming, sewing and cookery and in these situations readily accepted the need for order and organization. In one sense, they were learning as well as teaching. Thus, it appears fair to say that because of increasing involvement with parents, a healthier understanding on both sides has grown, leading to a more common form of order.

Self-discipline on the part of the children must be the first consideration of a school with such social aims, but over the years all concerned with them, whilst striving to encourage this attitude, have found how great are the difficulties inherent in this philosophy in such an area as ours. We have persistently tried to encourage independence, self-reliance and self-control, with various degrees of success. Our charges are plenteously endowed with the first two qualities. At the tender age of eight, many are mini parents with almost the sole responsibility for younger children; they continue to amaze and astound with their ability for self-entertainment and responsibility for valid tasks of a short duration. But as for self-control, this appears to be one sphere where environment and conditions conspire to make the majority of the children falter. In addition, parents tend to encourage their children to 'stand up for themselves' and do not present a sense of purpose in controlling their moods. Yet, as a strange contrast, I have never met children endowed with more body control in PE and games. On entering school, the tiniest infants are most able in climbing, throwing, kicking and most physical skills. It is obvious then that if self-discipline cannot easily be fostered, the controlling interest and discipline within the school must be exerted by trusted, stable, friendly adults.

The discipline of any school is an ongoing experiment in personal relations. It must be apparent that in my particular situation the constituents of the experiment have to be more carefully weighed, more critically balanced than in many other places, because of their sensitivity and volatility. But the experiment must succeed here if the true values and aims of the school are to be achieved. The problems are not to be minimized; they vary in intensity from day to day, but they must be honestly and fearlessly tackled. The interrelated roles of the children and adults, so important in the everyday running of the school community, need to be consistently reviewed, in order to attain maximum effectiveness and to avoid the dangerous state of self-satisfaction and, thence, stagnation.

The contributors

Gene Adams
Practising teacher and Secretary of STOPP

Rhodes Boyson
Headmaster, Highbury Grove Comprehensive, London

Robert Brooks
Senior Lecturer in Education, Brighton College of Education

Ronald Cocking
Headmaster, Colmers Farm County Junior School, Birmingham
Past President of the National Association of Schoolmasters

Michael Duane
Headmaster, Risinghill Comprehensive, London (Although the school
is no longer in existence, Michael Duane is still paid as headmaster.)

R. F. Mackenzie
Headmaster, Summerhill Academy, Aberdeen

Jack Reynard
Headmaster, St Margaret's C of E Primary School, Liverpool (at the
time of writing)
Deputy Director of Priority, National Centre for Urban Community
Education, Liverpool

Catherine Storr
Writer and mother

Barry Turner
Educational journalist and broadcaster

Keith Wadd
Head of Social Studies, Margaret McMillan College of Education,
Bradford

John Watts
Principal, Countesthorpe College, Leicester

Derek Wright
Senior Lecturer in Psychology, University of Leicester